PASTORING FOR LIFE

Theological Wisdom for Ministering Well

Jason Byassee, Series Editor

Aging: Growing Old in Church
by Will Willimon

Friendship: The Heart of Being Human
by Victor Lee Austin

*Recovering: From Brokenness and Addiction to
Blessedness and Community*
by Aaron White

Other Books by the Author

Calling and Character: Virtues of the Ordained Life

*Pastor: The Theology and Practice of Ordained
Ministry*

Accidental Preacher: A Memoir

*Who Lynched Willie Earle? Preaching to Confront
Racism*

Fear of the Other: No Fear in Love

AGING

> GROWING OLD
>
> IN CHURCH

WILL WILLIMON

Baker Academic

a division of Baker Publishing Group
Grand Rapids, Michigan

Published by Baker Academic
a division of Baker Publishing Group
PO Box 6287, Grand Rapids, MI 49516-6287
www.bakeracademic.com

Printed in the United States of America

Library of Congress Cataloging-in-Publication Data
Names: Willimon, William H., author.
Title: Aging: growing old in church / Will Willimon.
Description: Grand Rapids : Baker Academic, a division of Baker Publishing Group,
    2020. | Series: Pastoring for life: theological wisdom for ministering well | Includes
    index.
Identifiers: LCCN 2019031878 | ISBN 9781540960818 (paperback)
Subjects: LCSH: Older persons—Religious life. | Aging—Religious
    aspects—Christianity.
Classification: LCC BV4580.W525 2020 | DDC 248.8/5—dc23
LC record available at https://lccn.loc.gov/2019031878

ISBN 9781540962744 (casebound)

20 21 22 23 24 25 26   7 6 5 4 3 2 1

For my sister, Harriet, and my brother, Bud,
as they approach ninety with vitality

Contents

Series Preface

One of the great privileges of being a pastor is that people seek out your presence in some of life's most jarring transitions. They want to give thanks. Or cry out for help. They seek wisdom and think you may know where to find some. Above all, they long for God, even if they wouldn't know to put it that way. I remember phone calls that came in a rush of excitement, terror, and hope. "We had our baby!" "It looks like she is going to die." "I think I'm going to retire." "He's turning sixteen!" "We got our diagnosis." Sometimes the caller didn't know why they were calling their pastor. They just knew it was a good thing to do. They were right. I will always treasure the privilege of being in the room for some of life's most intense moments.

And, of course, we don't pastor only during intense times. No one can live at that decibel level all the time. We pastor in the ordinary, the mundane, the beautiful (or depressing!) day-by-day most of the time. Yet it is striking how often during those everyday moments our talk turns to the transitions of birth, death, illness, and the beginning and end of vocation. Pastors sometimes joke, or lament, that we are only ever called when people want to be "hatched, matched, or dispatched"—born or baptized, married, or eulogized. But those are moments we share with all humanity, and they are good moments in which to do gospel work. As an American, it feels perfectly natural to ask a couple how they met. But a South African friend told me he feels this is exceedingly intrusive! What I am really asking is how someone met God as they met the person to whom they have made lifelong promises. I am asking about transition and encounter—the tender places where the God of cross and resurrection meets us. And I am thinking about how to bear witness amid the transitions that are our lives. Pastors are the ones who get phone calls at these moments and have the joy, burden, or just plain old workaday job of showing up with oil for anointing, with prayers, to be a sign of the Holy Spirit's overshadowing goodness in all of our lives.

I am so proud of this series of books. The authors are remarkable, the scholarship first-rate, the prose readable—even elegant—the claims made ambitious and then well defended. I am especially pleased because so often in the church we play small ball. We argue with one another over intramural matters while the world around us struggles, burns, ignores, or otherwise proceeds on its way. The problem is that the gospel of Jesus Christ isn't just for the renewal of the church. It's for the renewal of the cosmos—everything God bothered to create in the first place. God's gifts are not *for* God's people. They are *through* God's people, *for* everybody else. These authors write with wisdom, precision, insight, grace, and good humor. I so love the books that have resulted. May God use them to bring glory to God's name, grace to God's children, renewal to the church, and blessings to the world that God so loves and is dying to save.

Jason Byassee

Introduction

One of my favorite photos of my namesake, Will, is of the two of us, he in his second summer of life on his first trip to the South Carolina coast. I'm leading into the surf at sunset one who only recently had learned to walk. I expected him to be afraid at his first meeting of the sea. He is no fear and all joy. He holds my hand. In the photo, you can see only our backs, an old man stooping toward the child, the child eagerly pushing forward. You can't see, but I'll never forget, the smile on his face, Will's delight as he eagerly entered the waves at my encouraging, "Jump!"

I love that photo's depiction of one of the great joys of aging—leading a little one toward the grand adventure of the wide world, gripping his hand reassuringly, egging him on to face into the wind and to leap the waves.

But yesterday, when I looked at that picture of the two of us—the little boy and the old man, the growing child and the aging adult—it occurred to me that I had misread that moment. I, who presumed to be leading the child, saw that I was being led. Here at sunset, the sea, the vast eternity of time that was rushing toward him with promise, was ebbing away from me, taking from me all that I loved, including the little boy named for me.

He was all future; I was now mostly past. Most of his life was ahead of him; most of my life was behind me. In truth, the little one, still fresh in the world, had me by the hand, encouraging me

1

to make my way into the deep, departing. He begins life by eagerly jumping forward. I clutch his tiny hand tightly, my last grasp of the future, at the end of day as I stagger uncertainly, unwillingly toward the engulfing, eternal sea. Not long from now, much sooner than I'd like, he'll have to let go and venture on without me. His grip is not tight enough to rescue me from the encroaching dark, the inundating deep.

When all is said and done (which will occur before long for this septuagenarian), there's no cure for that but God.[1] Just about everybody wants a long life; nobody wants to be old. Well, I'm growing old. So are you. Whether that's good news or bad depends not only on our physical and mental health, our financial situation, and our friends and family but also on the God who created us to be tethered to temporality and is our sole hope for resurrection.

"I grow old. . . . I shall wear the bottoms of my trousers rolled," I read at nineteen and snickered.[2] Aging is diminishment, finding yourself on the short end of life, with more yesterdays and fewer tomorrows, too small for your britches. Poet Dylan Thomas famously urged his aged father, "Do not go gentle into that good night. . . . Rage against dying of the light."[3] Is there somewhere to stand between stoic acquiescence and impotent wrath to the diminishment of aging before the gathering dark?

The day I began research on this book a colleague asked menacingly, "Ought not you to be thinking of . . . retirement?" I replied that I felt I was making a solid contribution to the school, my classes were well filled, and I expected to be teaching for a few more years. "But don't you think there's a time to back away?" she asked. Was the Lord behind this colleague's efforts to point this septuagenarian to the door? Maybe. All I know for sure is that the humbling conversation filled me with new enthusiasm for writing this book.

I write not only as a pastor, bishop, author, and theological educator but also as someone with personal experience of elderhood. I'm an aging Baby Boomer Christian. A widespread generational desire of us Boomers is to pioneer fresh ways of aging. A study of us Boomers approaching retirement by Princeton Survey Research Associates International found that we have "a vision of the post-midlife years that is inimical to the notion of decline, whether that be . . . pulling back gradually but steadily, or phasing out."⁴ This book is proof that we Boomers plan to age differently.

Ralph Waldo Emerson wrote his essay "Old-Age" at age fifty-seven. Simone D. Beauvoir wrote her rather depressing *The Coming of Age* at sixty. Cicero wrote his classic *De Senectute* at sixty-two. While I am not as smart as these earlier commentators on aging, I have one thing on them—I am actually old!

As a doctor looks at a sick man on his deathbed, shakes his head, and says, "He won't get over this," one could look into our crib, said Augustine in a sermon, and say on the first day of life, "He won't get out of this alive."⁵ Aging is a natural, predictable life process that imperceptibly begins at birth, accelerates in a few decades, eventually becomes undeniable, ends in death, and is the dominant factor in the last third of most people's lives. Natural and predictable though aging may be, let's be honest: one of the reasons aging requires courage is the looming, encroaching specter of death. Though mortality may have resided somewhere in our consciousness—as something unpleasant that happens to others—after sixty-five, most of us become more aware of what's next.

All of us are either participants or observers in a longevity revolution. Old age isn't as short as it used to be. If people retire at fifty, they can expect to spend nearly half their lives doing something other than their job. Just this week I read another book on the predicted doom of pension plans in North America (the crash comes in 2050). The reason for the coming pension crisis? People like me are refusing to die according to actuarial expectations. Genesis 6:3 defines maximum human longevity as "one hundred twenty years" (which is now the official maximum life span for humans). Psalm 90:10 more realistically says,

> The days of our life are seventy years,
>   or perhaps eighty, if we are strong. (NRSV)

Defying biblical marks for longevity, most of us will live thirty-four years longer than our great-grandparents.

During his earthly ministry, Jesus probably met few people my age. The average life span for men in the Roman Empire was twenty-five, probably less for women, and, as everyone knows, Jesus and many of his disciples were denied the opportunity to grow old.[6] Many of our quandaries about aging were unknown in biblical times or in the early church. However, that does not mean that Scripture, Christian theology, and local church life have nothing to contribute to our reflection on aging. As we think about aging *as Christians*, we should expect fresh insights and a fundamental reframing of what the world considers to be "the problem of aging."

Though any interest in math was killed in me by the time I hit junior high, even I can't talk about aging without first doing the numbers: In the United States the average life span is eighty, double that of two hundred years ago. Seventy million people will be over sixty-five by 2030, double today's numbers. Because women have a longer life span than men, American women beyond age seventy-five outnumber men three to one. The very old—those over eighty-six— are one of the fastest-growing age groups. This group numbered four million in 2000 and are projected to grow to nearly nine million by 2030 and to sixteen million by 2050. Centenarians increased from fifteen thousand in 1982 to well over one hundred thousand today. The aged segment of the population will grow from 12 percent to 21 percent, compared with 1900, when those sixty-five and over were only 4 percent of the population.[7] By 2058 the number of people sixty and older worldwide will triple to two billion, with aging persons comprising one-fifth of the world's population. Most will be living in rural poverty.

Dramatic changes in life spans have shifted our views of aging and our expectations for how adults function in the last quarter of life. The challenges of caring for the aged and the sheer size of the exploding aging population have made aging not only a major public policy dilemma and a disruption in millions of families but also an opportunity for Christians to rediscover the unique consolations and challenges that our faith has to offer in the last quarter of life.

Churches in North America are graying even faster than the general American population. Though there are few explicit resources in Scripture for aging, the Christian faith has the capacity to find fresh meaning in the last decades of our life cycle. After interviews and visits in dozens of congregations for whom ministry with the aging is a major part of their mission, I believe that Christians can prepare for the predictable crises of aging and that congregational leaders can be key to that preparation.

The Christian is commissioned to give testimony throughout the entire life cycle—including retirement, aging, sickness, and death—that God is faithful all the days of our lives. We can retire from our careers but not from discipleship; the church has a responsibility to equip us for discipleship in the last years of our lives. Even though growing old usually includes some painful events, the Christian faith can enable us to live through both the joys and the anguish of aging with confidence and hope.

Those who care for, work with, preach to, and counsel the exploding aging population need help to understand the aging process and its predictable crises as well as theological resources for speaking to aging persons and helping them to conceive of and negotiate the crises of growing old. This book hopes to help people answer the question, "Where is God leading me in this time of life?"

Some of us in my generation of aging Americans are the first to have the extraordinary financial resources that enabled us to retire earlier than ever imaginable for previous generations. For others, unaffordable health care, poverty, housing insecurity, and painful dislocation fill their last years with anxiety and fear. Many find that they are unprepared intellectually, emotionally, and spiritually for those years. Personal resolve and positive attitudes cannot rescue the aging from systemic injustices that make their last years of life anything but golden. This book is written to help Christians—the young who care for the aging and who are themselves preparing to age as well as those entering into and living through aging—think like Christians about elderhood and to see their congregations as ideal locations for ministry with and for the aging.

The median age of my own denomination is now sixty-two. "If you plan to be a Methodist preacher," I recently told a group of seminarians, "learn to love ministry with the elderly." Caring for and caring about, working with and understanding better, and offering compassionate support for the elderly and their caregivers have become a major mission opportunity. This book intends to offer biblical and theological reflection in conversation with some of the latest research on aging to provide specific, practical steps for congregations to engage in elder ministry. I hope that you will read this book as my joyful testimony that though working for and with Jesus can be daunting at any time of life, his light is our life and in his service is our joy, particularly toward the end of our lives.

Thanks to Carsten Bryant, who helped with the research and editing, and to Jason Byassee, who asked me for the book. My goal? To assist Christians to love God by honoring their elders and to help us prepare for aging like Christians so that we can die holy deaths.

ONE

Aging with Scripture

The most expensive advertisements on the nightly news tout drugs for the aging. Some drugs promise relief for the aches, pains, and illnesses of aging; other drugs swear they can stem the effects of growing old. In these ads, older adults appear peddling bicycles, bungee jumping, or gleefully splashing about in the pool with their grandkids. "Grow old along with me! / The best is yet to be."[1] We wish the exaggerated claims of these advertisements were true because when people are asked what comes to mind when they hear the term *growing old*, the majority respond not with words about golden years but with talk of loss, loneliness, dependency, grief, sadness, abandonment, dementia, and regret.

Somewhere between bungee jumping and despondent loneliness lies the truth of old age.

As Christians, we gather weekly in order to bend our lives toward an ancient text, a collection of writings that we believe to be strong evidence that God has graciously condescended toward us. Yet when we search the Scriptures, we find that the Bible's verdict on human aging is ambiguous.

Aging in the Old Testament

Well into his retirement, Billy Graham wrote a little book, *Nearing Home: Life, Faith, and Finishing Well*, in which he assembled his favorite Scripture passages related to aging.[2] While he found 175 references to elders in the Bible, even one so adept with the Bible as Graham had a tough time finding explicit biblical material that helps us think about elderhood—people didn't live very long in Bible times. There's also a theological reason for Scripture's relative lack of interest in aging: Israel and the church didn't place much stress on different ages and stages of life. Aging and dying were considered to be natural, expected, even providential processes that were ordained and guided by God rather than discrete chronological stages of human development.

It's possible that our negative and unrealistic attitudes about aging—as displayed in those pharmaceutical ads—are evidence of the North American church's cultural captivity, of Christians' capitulation to the mores and values of a culture that's not Christian. In a death-denial society, we the aging tell the young a tough truth even without intending to do so: we are everyone's future, whether they want to face it or not.

Graham notes that some Scripture passages look at longevity as God's reward for a life well lived. Proverbs 16:31 calls gray hair "a crown of glory" that "is found on the path of righteousness." The young have a duty to esteem their long-lived elders: "Honor your father and your mother so that your life will be long on the fertile land that the LORD your God is giving you" (Exod. 20:12).

Yet there is another side to old age. Graham calls Ecclesiastes 12:1–8 "one of the most poetic (and yet candid) descriptions in all literature of old-age."[3] I less charitably characterize this passage as beautiful but brutal.

> Remember your creator in the days of your youth, before the days of trouble come, and the years draw near when you will say, "I have no pleasure in them"; before the sun and the light and the moon and the stars are darkened and the clouds return with the rain; in the day when the guards of the house tremble, and the strong men are bent, and the women who grind cease working because they are few, and those who look through the windows see dimly; when the doors on the street are shut, and the sound of the grinding is low, and one rises up at the sound of a bird, and all the daughters of song are brought low; when one is afraid of heights, and terrors are in the road; the

almond tree blossoms, the grasshopper drags itself along and desire
fails; because all must go to their eternal home, and the mourners
will go about the streets; before the silver cord is snapped, and the
golden bowl is broken, and the pitcher is broken at the fountain, and
the wheel broken at the cistern, and the dust returns to the earth as
it was, and the breath returns to God who gave it. Vanity of vanities,
says the Teacher; all is vanity. (NRSV)

"Remember your creator in the days of your youth" sounds like the
advice of the old to the young. Attend the church youth group, study
Scripture every day, and obey God's statutes when you are young
because your youthful commitments are determinative of your later
faith. But then Ecclesiastes puts forth a more somber reason to be
with God in youth: "Before the days of trouble come, and the years
draw near when you will say, 'I have no pleasure in them'; before the
sun and the light and the moon and the stars are darkened and the
clouds return with the rain" (12:1–2 NRSV).

Though Graham doesn't even note these verses, Ecclesiastes is not
the cheeriest view of old age by a long shot. Ecclesiastes characterizes
the supposedly golden years as "days of trouble" in which, when the
sky turns dark and the light is dim, we are likely to look on the joys
of earlier days and say, "I have no pleasure in them." Kids, remember
your creator when you are young because when you are old, you will
despise God. What a thought to lay on the young!

Ecclesiastes also waxes grimly poetic in describing the aging body:
"the guards of the house tremble" (that is, your hands palsy), "the
strong men are bent" (your weak legs get crooked), "the women
who grind cease working because they are few" (your teeth fall out),
"those who look through the windows see dimly" (you are blind),
"the doors on the street are shut" (you are lonely), "the sound of the
grinding is low, and one rises up at the sound of a bird" (you never
get a good night's rest), "all the daughters of song are brought low"
(your voice is weak and trembling), "one is afraid of heights, and
terrors are in the road" (you are timid and fearful), "the almond tree
blossoms" (your hair is white), "the grasshopper drags itself along"
(you creak and stumble around), "desire fails" (need I spell this one
out?), "and the dust returns to the earth as it was, and the breath

returns to God who gave it. Vanity of vanities, says the Teacher, all is vanity."

I'm grateful that the canon kept the wisdom of Ecclesiastes, refusing to sugarcoat some of the realities of aging. Heap honor and gratitude on aging all you want, but you haven't told the truth about aging until you have done business with Ecclesiastes 12 and the Teacher's characterization of the troubled days.

Better think about God and the blessings of life when you are young because when the "days of trouble come" you may not want to be around God. These melancholy words from Ecclesiastes imply that more preparation is required for the rigors of aging than the accumulation of a hefty 401(k).

Aging in the New Testament

This negative side to the ambiguity of aging in the Old Testament seems less pronounced in the New Testament. While older adults are few in the Gospels or the letters of Paul, the elderly are major actors in the opening of Luke's Gospel. Luke believes that we can't get to the babe of Bethlehem without being led there by old people such as the priest Zechariah and his wife, Elizabeth, a childless older couple who are "very old" (Luke 1:7). The angel Gabriel appears to Zechariah and promises that Elizabeth will bear a son named John, bumping her from the geriatric ward to the maternity ward. Even in her old age, God calls this woman into faithful service. Zechariah finds this promise incredible due to their advanced age, but—wonder of wonders—embarrassed Elizabeth gives birth. Even though Elizabeth is old, she is the very first character in Luke's story to be "filled with the Holy Spirit" (v. 41). Elders become God's inspired instruments, commissioned interpreters to the Virgin Mary.

Next Luke introduces us to old Simeon and Anna, who welcome Jesus to the temple (2:25–38). Simeon hopes for the deliverance of Israel from oppression and, upon seeing the infant Jesus, proclaims Jesus as the chosen one who is the Deliverer. Throughout Luke, people have difficulty understanding who Jesus is and what he is up to. Is Simeon's astute perception of Jesus and Jesus's identity a function of the wisdom he has accrued over the years? Does Simeon see the child as God's rebuke to those who have given up hope for deliverance? Are older folks the first to get the astounding news of Jesus's birth because after many decades of living they are now unsurprised by the stunts of God?

Both Zechariah and Elizabeth and Simeon and Anna embody wisdom and insight—some gained through past experience, some as gift of the Holy Spirit. They are presented by Luke as prophets who point younger folks toward the future with expectation and hope. By the grace of God, they publicly, hopefully testify about tomorrow. Might Luke be suggesting that rather than being stuck in the past and unable to adjust to change, older adults who have been well-formed in the faith have a radical openness to the future and wise discernment of the times?

While many of us elders value continuity, tradition, and stability, it is striking that Luke connects older people to the possibility of unanticipated divine intervention. They have many years on them, but they point toward God's radical new future, as in, "Your young men shall see visions, and your old men shall dream dreams" (Acts 2:17 NRSV). In the outpouring of the Holy Spirit, the elderly are called to be dreamers. The Holy Spirit is a gift that keeps pointing the elderly toward visions of tomorrow rather than leaving them to wallow in memories of yesterday.

The Pastoral Epistles depict the early church as a place of respect for and honor of elders. First Timothy 5:1 says, "Do not rebuke an older man but exhort him as you would a father" (RSV). There are also specific directives to the community to provide assistance to widows. While the church owes elders honor and respect, it is noteworthy that responsible discipleship is expected from the elders. Older men like me, when necessary, can be exhorted. Widows are directed to devote themselves to prayer, hospitality, and service of the afflicted (vv. 3–16)—not only to be served but also to serve. Elders are called to be paradigms of faith and role models (Titus 2:2–5), teaching, counseling, and offering what guidance they can. Clearly, the New Testament authors consider elders to be worthy of special care yet still under Christ's vocational mandate to follow him as responsible agents.

After looking over the New Testament material on aging, Duke's Richard and Judith Hays note what is *not* said about older people in the New Testament: "Nowhere in the biblical canon are they pitied, patronized, or treated with condescension. Nowhere is growing old itself described as a problem. Nowhere are the eldest described as pitiable, irrelevant, or behind the curve, as inactive or unproductive. Nowhere are they, as in so many Western dramas and narratives, lampooned as comic figures."[4]

Even more remarkable, the New Testament, while calling death "the last enemy" (1 Cor. 15:26), does not consider death the worst thing that can happen to old people. The Hayses say that Jesus's death at an early age (he was no more than thirty-six) stands as a permanent reminder that fidelity is more important than longevity and that there is something worse than not living to a ripe old age.[5] Infidelity is a sin; mortality is not.

While long years are a blessing (Prov. 16:31; 20:29), a long life is not an inherent right, nor can it be the supreme goal of life. God, the giver of life, may call us to surrender our lives. The way of discipleship in the name of Jesus may not lead to a fruitful retirement but to the cross (Mark 8:34–38; Luke 14:25–27). I know a pastor who, on the verge of retirement, has been appointed to serve the most divided, difficult congregation of his entire ministry. Though his plan was to retire next year, he has committed to the bishop to stay at his post (in his words) "until this church gets healed of its craziness or I drop dead." I have many friends who, having enjoyed good health for most of their lives, are straining to offer a positive witness to the world even while under the burden of pain and sickness at the end of their lives. Discipleship, the way of the cross, is not for the faint of heart of any age.

Aging as Vocation

Researchers into successful aging stress the importance of seeing our last third of life as a time of continuing change and development. Some of these developments are necessitated by changing bodies and economic circumstances; others are precipitated by shifting social and familial relationships. Yet it's important for Christians to note that some of the change and development that's required in our last years is instigated by a living God who keeps calling us to witness, to testify, and to continue to walk the narrow way of discipleship. In John 3, we meet a man named Nicodemus who comes to Jesus by night. Though John doesn't tell us Nicodemus's specific age, when Nicodemus questions how a man can be born when he is old, Jesus responds that the Holy Spirit is able to provide new birth even among the aging. One is never too old to be rebirthed, made young again, sent on outrageous errands, or discombobulated by the Holy Spirit.

Because God isn't "the God of the dead but of the living" (Mark 12:27), our lives are subject not only to chronology and the possibility of mental and physical incapacity but also to a God who thinks nothing of constantly calling ordinary people—of any age—to follow him. A key question for each Christian is, "What is God doing in my life now?" Or more to the point of vocation, "What does God expect from me and to what tasks am I now being assigned?"

The God of the Bible who called people late in life—Elizabeth and Zechariah, Abraham and Sarah—keeps calling. Simeon blesses the young holy family and yet speaks a hard truth to Mary concerning the future of her son (Luke 2:34–35). Simeon and Anna show a boldness that characterizes some older people who, after a lifetime of responsible caution—keeping a job, being an example to their children—are now free to use their remaining precious time telling the truth—that is, being God's prophets. Though Anna is a person of great age, she is a truth-telling prophet in her last years. Perhaps this is the blessed, fruitful old age promised by the psalmist: "In old age they still produce fruit" (Ps. 92:14 NRSV).

Stuck in jail, Paul calls himself an old man, but still he expressed hope that he would be released for the express purpose of continuing his missionary vocation (Phil. 1:19, 22). This lifetime quality of divine vocation may explain why the only explicit reference to retirement in the Bible concerns the members of the tribe of Levi, who assisted in Israel's worship and began their work at age twenty, "and from the age of fifty years they shall retire from the duty of the service and serve no more" (Num. 8:25 NRSV). Though my colleagues can encourage me to retire from active teaching, no one can excuse me from my vocation except the one who called me.

The psalmist prays not for long life but for life long enough to tell future generations the truth about God:

> So even to old age and gray hairs,
>   O God, do not forsake me,
> until I proclaim your might
>   to all the generations to come. (Ps. 71:18 NRSV)

Billy Graham pointed me to an elder I'd never heard of: old Barzillai, who, at great risk to himself, provided food and shelter for King David and his men (2 Sam. 17:27–29). In gratitude for Barzillai's hospitality, David invited the old man to spend the rest of his days in the king's palace. Barzillai refused the king's hospitality, pleading, "How many years do I have left that I should go up with the king to Jerusalem? I am now 80 years old. Do I know what is good or bad anymore? Can your servant taste what I eat or drink? Can I even hear the voices of men or women singers? Why should your servant be a burden to my master and king?" (19:34–35). Barzillai was old enough to provide help to the king but too old (and too wise in his old age) to find much enjoyment in the king's palatial comforts.

Scripture is honest about the dependency that usually comes with old age, but I'm unsure if that dependency is viewed negatively or positively. As Jesus said to Peter, "Truly, truly, I say to you, when you were young, you girded yourself and walked where you would; but when you are old, you will stretch out your hands, and another will gird you and carry you where you do not wish to go" (John 21:18 RSV). This is probably a prophecy of martyrdom for Peter as an old man, but it can more generally apply to the rest of us. Aging requires a person to "stretch out your hands" and ask for help from others as well as to submit to be carried "where you do not wish to go." Dependency on the kindness of others is a curse only in a world that worships self-sufficiency.

Martha Nussbaum, one of our greatest living philosophers, says that in a culture that adulates youth, bodily perfection, potency, and independence, is it a wonder that the aged are the subject of "widespread, indeed, virtually universal, social stigma"?[6] *The Cambridge Handbook of Age and Ageing* criticizes our culture's bleak stereotypes of aging as a mere social construction "reflecting negative beliefs and attitudes about old age rather than any valid objective evidence concerning the quality of life of older people or their ability to make a positive contribution to society. . . . Ageism, then, refers to a process of collective stereotyping which emphasizes the negative features of ageing which are ultimately traced back to biomedical 'decline,' rather than backed up by empirical research."[7]

A negative view of elderhood does not come from Christian Scripture but is among the many cultural accommodations that the North American church has made to American culture. Ageism, like sexism or racism, is not only a social construction; it's a sin to be confessed.

John Calvin famously spoke of Scripture as the lens through which Christians look at ourselves and the world.[8] The ambiguity, the truthfulness, and the peculiarity of biblical views on aging speak to us of the distinctiveness of the church's witness on elderhood. The church ought to articulate and underscore the disparity between how Christians talk about the last years of life and how the world characterizes aging. We must demonstrate, in our congregational life, the difference that Christ makes in the way we age and in how we relate to and engage in ministry to and with the aging.

I have an acquaintance, a distinguished biologist who retired after a lifetime of teaching and research. I was surprised when he called me and said, "I need a suggestion of a good, readable biblical commentary. I was quite an enthusiastic young Christian, active in campus religious groups during college. But then there was graduate school, followed by my first teaching position. My wife never cared much for church. I drifted away, became focused on other matters. Now that I'm retired, I've got time to think more deeply about things. I want to read systematically through the Bible, paying closer attention and spending more time with some parts of it. Can you suggest a commentary that would help me?"

It's wrong to focus too much on the losses of aging without also noting the gains, such as the gift of "time to think more deeply about things." When we Christians go to Scripture, it's not usually to find answers to specific questions like, "How can I endure the last decades of my life?" Rather, we live with Scripture, regularly spending time with the stories of God with us, not primarily as a rule book or a set of answers but rather as an old friend, a companion on life's journey.

As with any old friend, we are patient with the friend's retelling of stories they have told us before. Sometimes there is joy in hearing familiar words that are beloved all the more for their familiarity. We delight to find passages that spoke to us during one stage of our lives speak differently now. Or we are surprised by biblical characters we failed to notice in previous trips through Scripture. (Have you noted either Simeon's or Anna's age on your previous encounters with the story of the nativity?)

We speak of a biblical "passage." Through Scripture, we travel from one place to another, guided, enticed, and urged on by the text. As we make our passage into and through elderhood, the Bible, once spoken of quaintly as "the Book of the Ages," can be a trustworthy guide and companion.

T W O

The Storm of Aging

When speaking of America's exploding aging population, we reach for meteorological metaphors. Health care providers face a "tidal wave" of needy elderly. An "avalanche" of increased longevity will sweep away pension programs and Social Security. An aging population is a "death tsunami" in which so many Americans will be dying that all institutions (especially mainline Protestant churches) will be drained of membership and financial support. Expect a "demographic earthquake" when younger generations will be overwhelmed by the burden of caring for the elderly.

For the aging themselves, the financial, psychological, mental, sociological, and spiritual challenges of aging can make it feel as if moving into the last decades of life is like being cast into a storm. A storm's a-coming. The unprepared will be swept away. Batten down the hatches!

To be sure, Scripture suggests that a Christian view of aging begins with gratitude that we've been given an undeserved gift that someone in the first century would find inconceivable. And yet a peculiarly Christian view of aging cannot end in gratitude but must move toward an honest admission that this last act of our lives is ambiguous both in its meaning and in our individual experiences, a time of both fruition and decay, fulfillment and loss, freedom and dependence. These qualitative challenges are now aggravated by a quantitative crisis: so many of us are aged.

Most want to live longer; few want to grow old. Like the Teacher of Ecclesiastes, many have regarded elderhood not as an unambiguous gift but rather as a morose, burdensome, meaningless finale. Ecclesiastes's gloomy heir was William Shakespeare, who famously characterized aging as the sad sixth and seventh acts in life's tragic drama that ends somberly with the loss of everything.

> All the world's a stage,
> And all the men and women merely players;
> They have their exits and their entrances,
> And one man in his time plays many parts,
> His acts being seven ages. At first the infant,
> Mewling and puking in the nurse's arms;
> And then the whining schoolboy, with his satchel
> And shining morning face, creeping like snail
> Unwillingly to school. And then the lover,
> Sighing like furnace, with a woeful ballad
> Made to his mistress' eyebrow. Then a soldier,
> Full of strange oaths, and bearded like the pard,
> Jealous in honor, sudden and quick in quarrel,
> Seeking the bubble reputation
> Even in the cannon's mouth. And then the justice,
> In fair round belly with good capon lined,
> With eyes severe and beard of formal cut,
> Full of wise saws and modern instances;
> And so he plays his part. The sixth age shifts
> Into the lean and slippered pantaloon,
> With spectacles on nose and pouch on side;
> His youthful hose, well saved, a world too wide
> For his shrunk shank; and his big manly voice,
> Turning again toward childish treble, pipes
> And whistles in his sound. Last scene of all,
> That ends this strange eventful history,
> Is second childishness and mere oblivion,
> Sans teeth, sans eyes, sans taste, sans everything.[1]

King Lear's Retirement

The bard who characterized old age as "second childishness and mere oblivion, sans teeth, sans eyes, sans taste, sans everything" wrote the most famous (and tragic) drama of aging, *King Lear*. After read-

ing *Lear*, poet David Wright wrote a poem that sees the play as a
warning.

> You can't trust the sweetnesses your friends will
> offer, when they really want your office.[2]

Lear's eventual fatal train of disintegration of self, family, and
friends is set in motion by his realization that he is getting old and
ought to retire. Lear resolves to divide his realm among his three
daughters but only after demanding that each of them outdo the
others in publicly proclaiming her love for him, boasting that he
will offer the largest share of his estate to the daughter who loves
him most. Goneril and her sister Regan take turns fawning over the
old man. Cordelia modestly refuses to say anything in response to
Lear's outrageous proposition. Lear fumes, "Nothing shall come of
nothing"[3] and promptly disinherits daughter Cordelia, taking her
share and dividing it among her sisters. When Goneril and Regan talk
together alone, they admit that their declarations of love were bogus.
Their real estimate of their father is that he is a foolish old man.

Initially, Lear looked forward to relinquishing the burdens of ruling, "to shake all cares and business off our state, confirming them
on younger years."[4] Yet he makes a mess of his retirement by fatally
rejecting Cordelia's love as well as the loyalty of his dear friend Kent.
When Kent protests Lear's treatment of Cordelia, petulant Lear banishes him. Observing the old man's appalling behavior makes us
wonder, "Is the king becoming senile, or is he plain crazy?"

In the climactic act 2, after relations between Lear and Goneril and
Regan have thoroughly deteriorated, Lear yields completely to his
rage, cursing his ungrateful daughters. Accompanied by his mock-
ing fool (now his sole companion), Lear rushes out of the familial
storm in the palace into a violent storm on the heath, where he rants
against his daughters and descends into raving madness, blaspheming
the gods who have failed him, loathing his own children, welcoming
death, and contemptuously dismissing life as an unbearably meaningless tragedy.

Nothing that I (or the author of Ecclesiastes) could say about the
melancholy of aging is as candid or as bleak as *King Lear*. Though

I am uncertain in what fashion Shakespeare was a Christian, and though the Christian faith appears to play no role in the lives of the characters in this epic drama, *Lear* is a helpful, if morose, conversation partner for Christian reflection on aging.

For many interpreters, *Lear* is little more than a nihilistic, dark depiction of the horrors of growing old. Old age is a pathless wasteland, a storm of unspeakable loss in which blind rage is an understandable, though impotent, response. Some point out that while Lear is childish, petulant, and resentful, mostly Lear is old. *Old* is the chief excuse given for the king's behavior by those few who manage still to love him: his friends Kent, Gloucester, and most especially the wise fool. *Old* is the charge made against Lear by his two elder disgusted daughters. "You see how full of changes his age is," Goneril says to Regan, citing Lear's "poor judgment" in banishing Cordelia. "'Tis the infirmity of his age," Regan replies, charitably.[5]

Old becomes Lear's excuse for why his life has careened out of control. Before growing old, Lear ruled; now he is ruled over, subject to mental and physical deterioration, humiliatingly aware that his end draws near. "Pray, do not mock me: I am a very foolish fond old man," Lear says in his final reunion scene with Cordelia, blaming the sad course of events on the curse of being old.[6]

Lear cherishes his family. He hopes that his daughters love him enough to care for him in his last days and is deeply hurt by his (foolish) belief that daughter Cordelia does not love him and (later) his conclusion that daughters Goneril and Regan don't either. After his bumbling and ranting, Lear goes out into the rain and the cold, though the weather is not the tempest that has driven him to this end. Lear is bested by the "storm" of aging, forced to acknowledge his impotency and loneliness and to spend his last days confronting the results of his own weaknesses.

True, few children go so far as to have their parent's eyes gouged out, but the manner in which Goneril and Regan abuse their father continues in the crime of elder abuse in our day. After Lear cruelly banishes Cordelia, responsibility for him falls to the two elder sisters, who are none too pleased. "If our father carry authority with such disposition as he bears, this last surrender of his will but offend us," Goneril says. "We must do something, and i'th'heat."[7] They instruct their servants to ignore their father's peevish and (to Goneril's mind) pointless demands. Regan shuts up her house when she hears that the old man is on his way for a visit. The daughters complain about what is (in their estimation) their father's excessive demand for servants, but one feels that they would complain about him and lock him out even without his one hundred knights. Finally, they close their gates to Lear, leaving him at the mercy of the storm. Good riddance to an unbearable burden.

Bastard son Edmund, in his sham letter to his brother Edgar, sees Lear's decline and divestment as an opportunity for his personal aggrandizement. "The younger rises when the old doth fall," says Edmund as he busily betrays his father to the Duke of Cornwall.[8] The old man's decline is an opportunity for his children to make their move on Lear's inheritance.

The play ends (depending on which version is used) with Edgar pronouncing, "The oldest have borne most. We that are young shall never see so much, nor live so long."[9] The young can't conceive of the horrible burdens of being old: sans teeth, sans eyes, sans children, sans everything.

This masterwork of Shakespeare leaves me with a question: What in Lear's aging leads to this tragedy? Philosopher Martha Nussbaum notes that many recent productions of *King Lear* portray Lear as an older adult who suffers from dementia. Nussbaum objects. That we must have the king afflicted with dementia may say more about our culture than about Lear.[10] There is nothing in Shakespeare's play to suggest that dementia is Lear's problem.

Lear's mistake is that he retires by *shedding responsibility but continuing to control*. Lear strides into aging as a proud, powerful, willful regent, obsessed with controlling his kingdom and its future. He ages as he lived—vainly attempting to exercise omnipotent command. The play is set in motion when Lear makes the equivalent of a living will. Before I die, Lear says, I will dictate the distribution of my world. I determine that my loved ones respond to me as I demand. I will "retire," but I will do so without relinquishing my determination of them.

Nussbaum notes that the powerlessness of aging is particularly devastating to a person like Lear, who has "been totally hooked on his own power and fantasized invulnerability."[11] As Lear's fool candidly says to him, Lear has foolishly made "thy daughters thy mothers,"[12] reducing Lear to a needy child of his own children. Because control has been the purpose of his life, Lear rages, not so much against the perils of old age but against the powerlessness that he experiences in old age. He is not living demented, without memory or in another reality; he is raging against his painful new reality, which has occurred not because he is old but because he is a control freak who has mismanaged his retirement. His "madness" is not really dementia; it is rage against his loss of control and his impotency to defend himself against his daughters' attempts to do him in.

Aging as a Test of Character

Still, it's not quite right to see Lear's troubles as stemming from his botched retirement. He is brought to grief by his character. Lear moves from being an omnipotent king to being an ordinary man, a father, a friend and equal, changes for which Lear is ill-equipped. He foolishly thinks he can give away all that he has and yet retain lordship over it, dramatically divest the burdens of responsibility and divide his estate while still exercising control over the life he previously so proudly enjoyed.

Was Lear prone to anger when he was younger? Lear is certainly a very angry old man, but much of his anger stems from his anguished frustration, not at being old but at finding himself dependent and vulnerable.

Retirement goes poorly for Lear, not because his retirement led to dementia or to the dissolution of his family and friends but because in old age Lear's flaws caught up with him. Full of pride, puffed up by an inflated ego, Lear divides his estate, but only after demanding that his children flatter him. When his best friend questions his actions, Lear curses him. Lear insists not only that his family look after him in his old age but also that they maintain him as if he were still king, parading with a retinue of a hundred knights before he finally storms out into lonely oblivion.

Dementia or mistakes in retirement planning are not Lear's problem; Lear is Lear's problem. While aging may not bring out the best or the worst in us, aging often magnifies tendencies that were present in our characters throughout our lives.[13] Sometimes it's only in our later years that our chickens come home to roost. Lear's pompousness and pride, his petulance and peevishness are made worse in a man who values power and control. If your major needs are control, independence, and power over your circumstances (I confess I'm guilty on all counts!), retirement and aging can be tough. With the predictable physical, social, financial, and emotional changes that occur in aging, control-hoarding people (like me!) are in trouble once they're members of the AARP.

Lear's aging could have gone differently. He could have made different decisions, could have listened to the advice of his friends, could have been more sensitive to the points of view of his children, or could have been more honest with himself about his retirement as the ending of one way of life and more hopeful about the beginning of another phase of existence.

On the heath—alone except for his faithful fool, stripped of everything he loves, and at his life's end—Lear is forced into brutal self-awareness. He repents of some of his earlier impetuousness, but his honest self-assessment comes too late.

Too late for Lear, but perhaps not too late for us. Was Shakespeare's intent in writing *Lear* to show, through this worst-case scenario, what aging need not be? We can see aging and retirement as "mere oblivion," "sans everything," or we can view this stage of life as a call for self-reflection, for life-course correction, and for the embrace of a new direction in relating to others and to the world in a different but not altogether unhappy way.

For Christians, aging can be a call for increased attentiveness to and engagement with God. We believe that in Christ we are not destined to end alienated from those we love, raging and impotent, cursing our fate, at the mercy of a violent storm that sweeps all away. The One who loved us into life loves us to the end. God is with us as we go into life's last age, transforming our fate into our destiny.

More than one Shakespearean actor has quipped that by the time one is old enough to have had enough experience to play King Lear, one is too old for the demanding role. Perhaps we, by the grace of God, can prove these actors wrong. By the time we attain Lear's age, can we arrive with the conviction that God is there to welcome us? We are not alone in the storm. There's a way to age well, *and* we don't have to do it alone.

"Have you prepared for your retirement?" the TV ads ask as they hawk financial planning services. What if Lear had begun to experience, perhaps even to enjoy, moments of being less in control? What if a friend of Lear's had been able to tell him, in a way he could hear, "You are kidding yourself if you think you can distribute your goods to your daughters and still have sovereignty over them"? What if Lear had asked for help in acquiring the new skills he needed to turn the disaster of his retirement into an opportunity to be a better person?

What if Lear had been part of a church that felt responsibility for helping him prepare for his retirement by candidly confronting him with the challenges of aging and then helping him practice some of the spiritual disciplines needed to negotiate this tricky time of life?

Furthermore, if Lear's downfall is due to flaws in character, those of us in the church—the people whom Stanley Hauerwas calls the "community of character"[14]—ought to take note. Changing when we are old is tough, but with a living, constantly intrusive, transforming God and a caring, truthful church of God, it's never too late to be born again and again. Some of the most important work the church does in us is preparatory: preparing us for loss and teaching us how to grieve, how to confess, and how to receive forgiveness, thus "equipping the saints for the work of ministry" (Eph. 4:12–16) so that we may walk into life's tempests with confident faith.

When I offered a former parishioner comfort after the death of his wife of forty-six years, he said, "Preacher, I've been preparing for this for a month of Sundays. All the sermons I've heard, all the Sunday school classes I've sat through—homework for the big exam. Now we're gonna find out just how well I've listened." Or as jazz artist Eubie Blake is commonly quoted as saying, "If I'd known I was going to live this long, I'd have taken better care of myself."

THREE

Retiring with God

Chronology is not very helpful in defining late adulthood, with many people maintaining high physical and intellectual functioning into their eighties. The age of sixty-five remains a powerful cultural marker since that's when Americans are eligible for Social Security benefits. While sixty-five is the conventional door into late life through retirement, it can be too late to think about the challenges of retirement.

"There are at least two major tasks to human life," says Franciscan priest Richard Rohr, thinking developmentally rather than chronologically. "The first task is to build a strong 'container' or identity; the second is to find the contents that the container was meant to hold."[1] Rohr emphasizes the importance of completing the first task well in order to engage the second: "You need a very strong container to hold the contents and contradictions that arrive later in life. You ironically need a very strong ego structure to let go of your ego. You need to struggle with the rules more than a bit before you throw them out. You only internalize values by butting up against external values for a while."[2]

Rohr characterizes the first half of life as a time of building purpose and direction in life and fulfilling commitments. The first half is "largely concerned about *surviving successfully* . . . establishing an identity, a home, relationships, friends, community, security, and building a proper platform for our life."[3] In the first half, one is a

"soldier" who is "very loyal to strict meritocracy, to his own entitlement, to obedience and loyalty."[4]

The second half of life is "falling"—a form of suffering, a failure,
a loss, or a stumbling. We must thoughtfully "fall into" this rather
than simply fall backward. This falling is usually something that happens to us rather than something we choose. The crucial thing, says
Rohr, is to use this time to clarify and to refine in order to see "the
task within the task" and to "recognize the intentions and motives
for what one needs to do."[5] What we call retirement is not so much
losing a job as taking on a new job.

Oliver O'Donovan sounds much like Rohr when he says that the
task of aging is moving from "realizing unexplored potential to making sense of accumulated experience."[6] Rohr teaches that we live out
our true selves in the second half of life when we attempt to live in a
way that integrates our first half of life by discerning what we need
to keep and what we need to let go. Rohr puts it this way: "How can I
honor the legitimate needs of the first half of life while creating space,
vision, time, and grace for the second? *The holding of this tension
is the very shape of wisdom.*" Rohr famously says that "the way up
is the way down, or if you prefer, the way down is the way up."[7]

The Challenges of Retirement

I fear that Rohr risks putting too positive a face on the losses of
aging. The bleakest cinematic depiction of retirement as a way down,
down, down is the first scene of *About Schmidt*. The 2002 film opens
with Jack Nicholson sitting in a stripped-down office, surrounded
by empty shelves and packed boxes, impassively watching an office
clock tick off the minutes until five on his last hour of his last day
at his last job. When the clock strikes five, Nicholson sighs, gathers
his few belongings, and silently walks out on life as he has known it.

After seeing *About Schmidt*, a friend called to say, "The movie
begins with the saddest scene imaginable, then tells the saddest story
about a sad retirement. Everybody on the way to retirement should
be required to see it. But be warned: there's a nude scene with Jack
Nicholson and Kathy Bates in a hot tub. Though you'll try not to,
you'll be unable to keep yourself from looking."

About Schmidt depicts retirement as more than a tragedy: retirement pushes the protagonist into a journey of self-discovery, some of it painful, much of it exhilarating, as he finds a new life for himself. While retirement may not be the very best time in life, by God's grace, retirement need not be the worst.

Still, for many who are aging, as for King Lear, life's most difficult decades begin at sixty-five. Most suicides are by men; the highest rates for male suicide begin at fifty and continue to rise through age seventy. In this decade American suicide rates for men and women over fifty have risen markedly.[8] Keep those stark figures in mind the next time you hear sentimental claptrap about retirement.

Retirement isn't what it used to be. The median age for retirement in America declined to fifty-seven in the early 1990s from a high of seventy-four in 1910, when the expected life span was about fifty and neither Social Security nor pension plans existed.[9] Those who did not die at fifty continued to work because they had no choice; retirement was an unknown concept. Today's median retirement age is about sixty-two. Only a small percentage of Americans (5–10 percent) work beyond age seventy.[10] Voluntary retirement becomes more attractive when we have both critical masses of retirees with economic security and social expectations that retirement is a positive experience.

Differences in class, race, gender, and economic security that separate us throughout life become even larger and more detrimental in our last years. To speak of the elderly without accounting for those differences falsifies the subject. Still, we have learned much about general paths of aging, and these insights can inform a broad range of congregations who want to help members negotiate the challenges of retirement.

When workers are forced to stop working earlier than planned or earlier than they want, retirement is seen as a curse rather than a privilege. Compulsory retirement is an arbitrary and unnecessary rule that's usually based on age discrimination stereotypes rather than on careful evaluation of what a person is contributing to the company. The main function of compulsory retirement rules is to protect administrators from having to make informed and sometimes painful assessments and decisions about employees.

I know of a medical center where doctors were forced to retire at seventy. Mandatory retirement made sense to some of the doctors, who expressed gratitude that the institution made a decision about their retirement for them. Others, varying across their particular fields of medical practice and their personal abilities, pushed back. Some medical residents testified to the value of having a few experienced, wise practitioners to train them in diagnostics. The medical center decided to end mandatory retirement at seventy and to institute yearly reviews of all doctors over seventy, making retirement decisions on a case-by-case basis.

When my theological mentor, Karl Barth, was forced to retire from his faculty position in Basel, he moved his seminar to a local tavern, where the students flocked to receive Barth's wisdom.

Work—getting up, going out, and making a contribution to the larger good—is our major means of social interaction. Work keeps us active and in touch with the young. Ceasing from work thus presents the former working adult with a challenge: How shall I stay in contact with and keep exercising responsibility for others now that I no longer have a job to decide for me? What is the rationale for getting out of bed in the morning?

The Work of Retirement

In his book *Finding Meaning in the Second Half of Life: How to Finally, Really Grow Up*, James Hollis, using Rohr's two-part life schema, says that success in the second half is often dependent on the work we've done in the first. The first half accrues "growth, purpose, and meaning," which will be used to negotiate the challenges of the second half.[11] "What does the world ask of me, and what resources can I muster to meet its demands?" sets the agenda for the first half.[12] Hollis says that the "fantasy of acquisition" dominates the first half, "gaining ego strength to deal with separation, separating from the overt domination of parents, acquiring a standing in the world, whether it be through property, relationship, or social function," and building "a sense of ego strength sufficient to engage relationship, social role expectations, and to support oneself."[13]

The primary task of successful retirement is somehow coming to the realization that retirement is not only giving up and ending a way of life but also finding a passage from one form of life to another. It is possible for a person moving into the second half to see that retirement from one set of responsibilities and cares frees them to explore another set of obligations and to assume another set of concerns. We are surprised to find that as our time grows shorter, sometimes our time to explore ourselves and our world expands.

Retirement calls us to assume new narratives, moving from the story "I used to work, but now I have stopped working" to "Once I did this work and then I stopped doing it, so I am now free to do other work."

Let's be honest. Some of us retire from jobs that are meaningless. In our working years we may have invested too much in our jobs, attempting to imbue significance in a job that the job could not bear, vainly trying to receive satisfaction from a career that delivered little joy. Now, in retirement, we are free not to expect so much meaning from a rather meaningless job and to assume more fulfilling work.

Yet moving from working at a job into the jobs of retirement is not only movement into another stage of life; retirement is undeniably a movement into the last stage of life. We have not merely endured the bodily changes that come with the acquisition of years; we are entering the final years. This means we are no longer members of the generation in charge, which may be very painful to those of us like Lear who have derived a great deal of meaning from having authority and influence. Having observed the retirements of a number of fellow clergy, I know that the sidelining that accompanies aging may be most difficult for those who have enjoyed being at the center of attention. The worst part of retirement, confessed a retired Methodist pastor, "is that I've got just as much to say but no longer have that blessed twenty minutes every week to say it in a sermon."

It is possible for retirement to be liberating for those who have borne the heavy burdens of being in charge. I was cast by the church into a demanding job with heavy responsibility for the lives of others. Having retired from being bishop, I now enjoy having more choice over my areas of responsibility. While retirement is the loss of certain sorts of power, it can also entail the acquisition of different, more enjoyable empowerment.

If it is true, as it was for Lear, that one of our greatest fears in aging is loss of control, perhaps we ought to prepare ourselves for that inevitable eventuality. We should look for those occasions when we can be dependent, when we can put ourselves in the care of others and relax and go with the flow. We manage fear by facing our fears and by experiencing fear-inducing circumstances. Might we treat our fear of lack of control the same way?

"This Thanksgiving for the first time I'm going to sit back and let my daughter-in-law handle coordination and preparation of the family's Thanksgiving dinner," a woman proclaimed. "It's her trial run for taking charge when I'm not responsible for Thanksgiving the rest of my days."

The Economics of Retirement

Christianity is an embodied, incarnational faith. We Christians demonstrate our unique brand of spirituality when we concern ourselves with economic matters and with questions about the just distribution of God's material gifts. It would be tempting to talk about aging either as a mostly bodily and medical change or as a purely emotional, psychological, social, or attitudinal challenge. Yet the Christian faith—in the eternal Word became flesh (John 1:1)—will not allow us to act as if the economics of aging is beyond the bounds of theological concern. Body and spirit, the mundane and the divine, are joined in Jesus Christ.

I interviewed a woman who works as the coordinator of her town's senior center. She provides a marvelous network of social services for the aged.

"What's one thing that would improve the lives of the aged with whom you work?" I asked.

"For most of them, two hundred dollars a week would dramatically improve their situation," she replied. Some of the problems we treat as psychological, medical, or spiritual are economic.

Aging exposes and aggravates economic inequalities a person has endured for decades. A widespread social injustice in our country is the gap between the affluent aging and the nonaffluent aging. More than a third of the private wealth in the United States is held by 1 percent of the population, as aging Bernie Sanders says, and the elderly are overrepresented in this 1 percent group.[14] However, the majority of older adults have insufficient savings to meet even a modest medical or economic emergency, and most will need assistance from government, friends, and family. Almost a majority of Americans have no retirement savings (though many have equity value in their homes). Nearly 4 percent of Americans have no Social Security benefits to aid them in their last years.[15]

Aggravating these inequities is an economy that makes being in community difficult and turns our purportedly civilized society into Thomas Hobbes's *bellum omnium contra omnes*, a war of all against all. We assume that the best senior care is best offered by the best paid professionals, that there's not enough to go around, and that the source of good care is a well-designed economy. By feeding us a narrative that we are what we produce, a capitalistic culture can leave those no longer contributing to the GDP feeling purposeless and extraneous. Inherently adaptive, market driven, and innovative capitalism is at odds with those whose main contribution is passing on, nurturing, and protecting tradition. If productivity, rationality, and efficiency are considered to be the prime human contributions, then there is little for the aging to do. Elders become functionless and redundant. In a traditionalist or at least tradition-loving society, the old have something to contribute to the young, something the young do not have that can be given to them only by the old. When the aging are viewed as noncontributing, they are dismissed as those who are full of boring, irrelevant, repetitious stories that nobody wants to hear.

On the contrary, Deuteronomy 6 arises out of a culture that values the contributions of the aged. The way of the Lord is given to Israel, but the Lord knows that God's people will need one generation teaching another in order to keep the way of the Lord refurbished in the hearts of the people: "In the future, your children will ask you, 'What is the meaning of the laws, the regulations, and the case laws that the LORD our God commanded you?' Tell them: We were Pharaoh's slaves in Egypt. But the LORD brought us out of Egypt with a mighty hand. Before our own eyes, the LORD performed great and awesome deeds of power against Egypt, Pharaoh, and his entire dynasty" (vv. 20–22). A tradition-valuing, transgenerational culture says that the function of elders is to recite and to teach God's ways to the young.

The maximum annual Social Security benefit for a single person who retires at age sixty-six is a little less than $32,000. Most recipients don't qualify for the maximum benefit. The average benefit is about half that. The cost of living for an older single person who rents a residence is about $24,000. Social Security comprises about 90 percent of income for 22 percent of older couples and for 45 percent of older singles.[16] While these Americans may not be in danger of starving, they will testify that their lives are severely circumscribed by a lack of funds.

Only about half of households with people over sixty-five enter retirement with savings. Half of those households have a defined benefit retirement plan apart from Social Security, and 36 percent live in a mortgaged home. This means that about 60 percent of older Americans are categorized as poor on the basis of income. When home equity is considered, the home equity for older Americans at the poverty level is about $120,000, so about 10 percent of the forty million Americans over age sixty-five fall below the poverty line.[17]

The economics of retirement looks vastly different for the affluent. During the past couple of decades, some of the elderly have become much richer, while younger adult cohorts have become poorer. Many older Americans did well for themselves in their housing and in the stock market and stashed away more of their earnings than those who follow them. While their younger cohorts are still making money in their work, there is a widespread sense that the elderly are generally more affluent and are fiercely protective of their government benefits (called "entitlements" by conservative politicians) from any legislated diminution. By working longer than other generations, many Boomers are not leaving room in the job market or for advancement for younger generations. Many elderly voters have a conviction that if their fellow older adults are in need, they are in need because they foolishly failed to prepare financially for their retirement.

Social Security taxes are a major means of equalizing some of the wealth disparity in the United States. Most Social Security benefits are subsidized by the young because they are paid for by future taxes.

Social Security taxes are now about 6.2 percent, with another 6.2 percent paid by an employer on the first $18,000 of income.[18] Social Security is the primary way America forces people to save for retirement. It would seem to be good government policy to do everything we can both to encourage and to require people to prepare for their post-earning years. Therefore, it may be a Christian responsibility to vote for an expanded Social Security system, both in funding and in future benefits. While preparation through Social Security may be repugnant to those who favor smaller government and less government benefits, this could be the easiest way to help the indigent elderly and to relieve some difficult generational stresses in the future.

Critics of Social Security and Medicare blame the deterioration of care for families and children on the "graying" of the federal budget. It's true that by the 1980s, more than half the federal domestic budget was being spent (mostly through Social Security) on the elderly.[19] Older voters were accused of placing the financial burdens they were incurring on their children and grandchildren; the hard-earned tax dollars of the young were being spent on unduly golden retirements of the elderly. The 2018 tax reform gives some credence to this point of view. Republican tax policy reformed the taxation structure by preserving benefits for the elderly, by postponing and ceasing environmental protection, and by incurring massive debt for future generations of Americans. Those who lament the alleged "graying of American political power" (Trump is my age, though his coiffure has escaped this graying trend) have some evidence on their side. We elderly are voting for those who promise to protect our retirements, to shore up the present without much thought for the future, and (without admitting it) to pass on the bill to our grandchildren.

Legacies and Estates

King Lear is a warning to us that one of our most fateful decisions related to retirement concerns our legacy. Retirement and the prospect of the end of our lives brings out the worst and the best in us, magnifying our faults and our virtues. We need not have as large an estate as Lear's to do, like the raging king, great damage. Sometimes, the smaller the estate, the more fierce the family battle. Despite my pastoral efforts to work reconciliation, a brother and a sister to this day refuse to speak to each other because their mother's cherished bedroom dresser was given to one and not the other.

Frequently, a vain or lonely parent, like Lear, comes to view adult children as those with hands outstretched waiting for the parent to die and the will to go into effect. The parent is then tempted to threaten to withhold resources in order to gain more attention from the children. On the other hand, an adult child who nurtures memories of past pain inflicted by the parent or resentments arising from the burden of caring for the parent in their last years may view the parent's estate as the just restitution to which they are entitled, as did Lear's greedy daughters, Goneril and Regan.

A couple had a little farm that they lovingly nurtured throughout their lives, often saying, "This will belong to our children when we die." When both of them died within a few months of each other, I watched their surviving children squabble and put the farm up for auction to strangers rather than see any one sibling occupy the land. Their parents' funerals were the last gatherings of the family.

"John and Mary worked so hard to leave that farm to their children," someone in the church said, "only to have that farm, after their deaths, become the undoing of their family."

When my wife, Patsy, and I met with our attorney to draw up estate plans, our attorney said, "Do what you want with what you leave behind, but as for me, having seen so many otherwise good children ruined by the prospect of a rich inheritance, having seen so many families torn apart by fights over the estate, I'm telling my own children that they will receive a reasonable part of my estate, but I'm settling most of what I've got on a community foundation."

Realizing that as Christians we are under a mandate more demanding than the "family first" credo, that loving our grandchildren is not the extent of our ethical responsibilities, Patsy and I took the largest portion of our estate and formed a charitable foundation to be administered by our heirs when we're gone. We've provided for our children (most parents, if able, do that), but after we're dead, we hope to dispose of our property like Christians and provide for someone else's children.

This aging generation will leave behind the largest transfer of wealth ever. Whereas some of the elderly suffer from poverty, others bear the responsibility of estates. A big estate can lead elders to suspect that their loved ones are treating them well because of their expectation of a future reward, not because they love them. A large estate can also bring out bad behavior in elders as they make excessive, Lear-like demands on their children, saying, "Act as I command or you're out of the will."

Transference of accumulated wealth raises ethical questions for older people with means. Should we wait until death to dispose of our financial holdings? In our estate planning, should we strive for equality in passing on resources to our children, treating each heir equally? A good case can be made for distributing earthly goods (and an estate is nothing more than that—*earthly*) sooner rather than later. Once we have accumulated enough to support ourselves into old age, why not experience the joy of parting with as much of our resources as possible now, rather than putting it off until after our deaths?

Perhaps Warren Buffett and Bill and Melinda Gates, with their intentions to distribute their vast wealth beyond the bounds of their families, should be our models. Parental generosity can be a witness to our children: as a Christian, nothing that I have is exclusively mine; I deserved none of it, as everything belongs to God. Jesus rearranges our notions of family and has given us responsibility for the needs of others beyond the bounds of our biological kith and kin.

In our distribution of portions of our estates to our families, should we consider the differing needs and abilities of our children and grandchildren? The principle of perfect equality isn't much of a guide. God gives us the gift of discernment. Most parents love all their children equally but also distinctively, honoring each child's needs and gifts. On the one hand, perhaps we should distribute according to need, giving more resources to the adult child who has a child with special needs or to the child who has had less economic opportunity than the others. On the other hand, such unequal distribution can be tricky, as children may feel that their siblings have jockeyed for this special treatment through fake displays of filial affection. *King Lear* is a cautionary warning of the dangers of unequal distribution of an estate to one's children. Is your family one of sufficient honesty and Christian formation that you can distribute your estate unequally without fostering resentment?

Freedom *for* Rather than Freedom *From*

We have good reason to fear the trials of retirement. Being forced by retirement to quit the work that gave us meaning and purpose raises the fear that we will be lost without it. Downsizing to a smaller home in a different neighborhood means saying goodbye to people we have enjoyed. Will we be able to muster a reason to get out of bed each morning? Will we have value to anyone any longer? Retirement's accoutrements can include concerns about being cast exclusively with other older people and thereby segregated from younger generations, worries of financial insecurity, and FOMO—that is, the fear of missing out, for those of you not hip to Millennial acronyms. No wonder anxiety rises at the prospect of retirement.

Yet following Scripture's twofold sense that aging is not only a sometimes challenging, difficult time of life but also a divine blessing, we also must celebrate retirement's gifts. It is a sad commentary on our inadequate theology that we cannot affirm retirement's grant of blessed Sabbath rest. Most of our forebears would gladly have exchanged their burdens of having to work until they dropped for our First World retirement dilemmas. Here is a short list of some of the blessings of retirement: availability to help children and grandchildren, time to reconnect with friends and family, release from the burden of having to hold things together in a job, time to communicate with letters and email, extrication from some of the annoying hassles of working life, flexibility to sleep whenever desired, freedom to read and learn new things, liberty to say yes and no to offers, and opportunity to travel.

More than one early retiree has been surprised at receiving disapproval and even hostility from their coworkers, as if those who are still working said, "What gives you the right to turn your back on the career for which I'm making so many sacrifices and to which I'm giving my life?" Though the early retiree didn't mean for their retirement to be a critique of the work life of others, it was perceived in that way.

Freedom from work requires us to answer, "What am I now free for?" When we were actively working, our time was in the hands of others. We didn't spend much time asking, "What will I do today?"

In retirement we are free to "take time," which means not only free-dom but also new responsibility. If a person has had demanding, time-consuming work, having so much discretionary time can be a burden. One is now in a period of indeterminate length without an agenda imposed by society, faced with an array of choices about how to use time and resources, how to find purpose, and how to maintain relationships.

Odd that we often think of youth's "growing up" as a matter of accepting responsibility for the course of their lives when "growing old" is equally demanding, requiring us to be responsible for the use of our time as the time of our lives grows shorter, placing on us a sense of urgency to use well the time we have left. At work, we did not have to concern ourselves with what to do with time or find people with whom to interact: all that was readily available, done for us. Thus, retirement creates uncertainty and forces us to plan, to choose, to take responsibility. Retirement can be a time of new beginnings and a revival of interests that we had to put on the shelf in earlier life. Some retirees experience a new sense of urgency—time is limited, and if we are going to accomplish our goals, we had best begin now if we are to catch up with things, invest ourselves to the fullest, deal with unfinished business, overcome some perceived deficit in personality, or expand our horizons. In short, the bucket list syndrome.

What Paul said to new Christians ought to be said to those of us entering retirement: "You have stripped off the old self with its practices and have clothed yourselves with the new self, which is being renewed in knowledge according to the image of its creator" (Col. 3:9–10 NRSV). Retirement doesn't so much take away our self as it gives us a different sort of self. Having spent so much time exercising creativity—making, doing, achieving—we are now free to imitate our Creator in taking creative Sabbath rest.

Kenneth Calhoun wrote a delightful story, "Nightblooming," that tells of a young, aspiring jazz musician who encounters a group of older adults who "found themselves retired" and who reacted to their retirement by saying, "Now's finally the time to form a band!"

> You should see the instruments they fished out of attics and basements. Not so much the instruments themselves—horns haven't changed

much over the years—but the cases. Some are covered with flesh-tone leather, boxes made of wood with rusty hinges, lined with red velvet. When they crack them open, it looks like they're pulling metal bones from the insides of a body.

The dudes are severely elderly, these Nightblooming Jazzmen. They wear white belts and bow ties, polyester pants pulled up high. Our angle is we're old, they say.[20]

The Nightblooming Jazzmen have found that a chief gift of retirement is *freedom from* in order to be *free for*. Go ahead, form a jazz band, be like George W. Bush and take up painting, travel, or sit on a rock and look down on the valley. You are free. True, for Christians, freedom is a contested concept. We are never truly free, if freedom means the freedom to live only for ourselves. As Christians, we are baptismally named, claimed, called, attached, and commissioned by Christ. Our "freedom" may therefore be freedom from the cares entailed in our vocation (needing to earn money, care for our families, etc.) in order to have freedom for our chief Christian vocation—discipleship.

In an interview with her oldest grandson, Senator Barbara Boxer said, "I am never going to retire; the work is too important. But I am not going to be running for the Senate in 2016."[21]

For one faithful person, retirement freed him from his career so he could devote himself more fully to his vocation. The week after he retired from his engineering job, he offered himself for service to the church, saying, "Now that I no longer have a job, I'm free for full-time Christian service." That's the spirit!

Preparing for Retirement

During my time as a pastor, I wouldn't perform the marriage of a couple I had not counseled. The purpose of this time of reflection together was not to tell them what they were getting into. How would I know that? My goal was to help them think about marriage as Christians. We talked about marriage as living out the implications of their baptism. I asked them how their marriage would support and encourage their vocation to discipleship.

What would it mean for me as a pastor to prepare the people of my congregation for retirement? The most successful retirement is premeditated in order to take full advantage of a recent privilege of a small portion of humanity. How can the church help folks think about retirement as Christians? As a preacher, my job is "to equip the saints [of any age] for the work of [all sorts of] ministry" (Eph. 4:12 NRSV). A main means of equipping is preaching, week in and week out, forming people whose faith in Christ enables them to negotiate the challenges of following Jesus. Through preaching, the Christian story is laid over our stories; we learn to look at life through the lens of Scripture. We thereby think like Christians, radically reframing words such as *freedom*, *dependency*, and *control* in light of Jesus Christ and his mission.

After the death of her husband, which was preceded by the deaths of both of her parents, a woman said to me, "I never noticed how much of Scripture is concerned with the plight of widows and orphans. Now that I'm both widowed and orphaned, I'm a more astute Christian than I was before. Life shoved me to the center of the Christian faith."

As I moved toward retirement, I received invitations from my bank and my employer to participate in preretirement planning. All these seminars focused on financial management. Why didn't my church gather some of us to think like Christians about this life transition?

As a pastor, I always convened my graduating high school seniors for an evening of pizza and discussion of the topic "Being Christian in College." That evening I unashamedly offered them "Rules for Staying Christian on Campus." I asked them, "What information, insights, or support do you need from your church as you launch forth into college?" I suggested that they promise God and themselves that they would read the Bible at the same time each day, pray daily, join a campus Christian group, keep in touch with their pastor during their first days in college, and so forth. Why didn't I convene my senior church members and instigate a similar conversation about their impending retirements?

Part of the pain of aging is being disconnected from the rituals that gave our lives meaning and order. In a period of life with many transitions, the patterned, predictable, purposeful ritual life of the church can take on greater meaning for us. Can't the church do better than the world's sorry rituals for retirement?[22] When students left for college or on a family's last Sunday as part of our congregation before they moved, we ended the service with a time of blessing in which we formally bid farewell and Godspeed and then laid on hands. Why didn't we do something similar to bid people into the adventure and the tasks of retirement? When someone in my church was thrown into the tasks of bereavement, I would routinely visit them in their home to see if I could be of help. Why didn't I pay them a pastoral visit when they retired from their work to hold them accountable to their vocation?

A SERMON

Here is a sermon I preached some years ago in an attempt to help my congregation think about retirement in a specifically biblical, Christian way.

Retirement: A Whole New Life[23]

Vanity of vanities, says the Teacher.
   . . . All is vanity.
What do people gain from all the toil
   at which they toil under the sun?
A generation goes, and a generation comes,
   but the earth remains forever.
. . . .
   There is nothing new under the sun. (Eccles. 1:2–4, 9
   NRSV)

Then I saw a new heaven and a new earth, for the first heaven and the first earth had passed away, and the sea was no more. . . . And the one who was seated on the throne said, "See, I am making all things new." (Rev. 21:1, 5)

My text is from Ecclesiastes, one of the Bible's most depressing, cynical books. "Vanity of vanities, says the Teacher. . . . All is vanity."

Have you ever felt like that, looking back on your life? Your accomplishments crumble in your hands as dust. Your great achievements appear as so much chasing after the wind.

No wonder the writer of Ecclesiastes feels this way about his life. "There is nothing new under the sun," he says. Life is just one thing after another, a great wheel in which there is no beginning and no end. Life is, in Shakespeare's words, full of "sound and fury, signifying nothing."[24] Ecclesiastes is one of the only books in the Bible with a cyclical view of history. History doesn't begin or end; it's not going anywhere. History is a great cycle, a circle. There is nothing new under the sun. When there is no ending or beginning, no real newness, life is depressing.

Everyone here will, some of you sooner than later, in some fashion, retire. Let's talk about retirement. I have a problem right from the start. When I preach, I like to preach from the Bible, take a biblical text and work from there. Trouble is, only recently did humanity live long enough or accumulate enough goods to "retire" in our sense of the word. The Bible, particularly the Hebrew Scripture, considers old age, a long life, a great gift of God. But retirement, what to do with our old age or our now widespread long lives, is a relatively recent problem.

I'm unhappy with the word *retirement*. It's a cousin of similarly uninspiring words like *retreat, remove, regress*. Retirement makes it sound as if, in our last years of life, we withdraw from the fray, settle in, settle down, quit moving, quit living, for all intents and purposes. Yet we're learning that each stage of life has its challenges, its different demands and new adventures, including retirement.

I recall a student whom I was teaching in seminary. He was serving his first little church as a student pastor. One day he complained to me about his congregation. "The median age of my congregation is over sixty," he declared. "And you know how old people are."

"How are they?" I asked.

"You know—set in their ways, creatures of habit, slow to change, stuck in their ruts. They don't want any innovation or change in the church."

Not two days before I had read an article on retirement that noted that, of the six or eight most difficult transitions you must make in life, the most traumatic changes, four or five of them will occur after sixty-five. Transitions like declining health, loss of independence, unemployment, and the loss of a spouse are among the major moves of this last stage of life.

I noted this information to the young student pastor, adding, "Which suggests that it's not fair to say that these older people are refusing to change. They are drowning in some of the most dramatic changes in life. When you've buried the man you have lived with for forty years, or you are forced out of your life work, about the last thing you want is to come to church and have some upstart young preacher say, 'Let's do something new and innovative this morning.' They're sinking in a flood of innovation!"

Bury the woman you lived with for forty years, wake up the next morning unmarried, that's innovation aplenty.

We once thought of adulthood as that time in life when you at last put down roots, hunkered down, burrowed in for the rest of your life, and stayed put. The really important developmental events occurred in infancy, childhood, or youth. We now know that adulthood is best construed as a series of passages (thank you, Gail Sheehy), of shifting challenges that are far from stable.

For some years I have taught a course to first-year students at Duke called "The Search for Meaning." We study the ways various people have found meaning in their lives, a reason to get out of bed in the morning. Students are pushed to articulate their own sense of meaning in life, to write down where they are headed and who they plan to be when they grow up.

I have noted that most of them think to themselves, "I'm all confused and in flux now, but when I am twenty-five, I will have decided who I want to be. I'll settle down, settle in, buy a minivan, vote a certain way, and be fixed forever."

Life is not like that. For instance, I note how odd it is for us to ask students, "What do you plan to do when you graduate from Duke?"

They respond with a sense of finality: "I'm going to be an electrical engineer." Or "I'm going into medicine."

But then we note that the average American goes through *seven* job changes in a lifetime. Someone from the Engineering School told me the other day that they did a study of their graduates and only 30 percent of them were in engineering twenty years after graduation!

See my point? These students had better be preparing for a more challenging life than merely figuring out what they want to do for the rest of their lives and expecting to stay in that job, fixed with that identity for the rest of their lives.

Is that why increasing numbers of educators are coming to speak of intelligence not in terms of IQ, a fixed intellectual quotient in you since birth, but rather intelligence as *the ability to adapt*? Life is this long series of adaptations, moves, changes, beginnings, and endings, some of them precipitated by the changing state of our bodies, some due to cultural shifts, and some due to the machinations of a living God.

As a pastor, I've watched a good number of people move into retirement. I'm on my way there myself. And though, from what I've observed, there are a number of challenges in the allegedly "golden years," one stands out above all the rest: *retirement is a whole new life*. I'm here paraphrasing from a great book by my friend Reynolds Price, *A Whole New Life*.[25] It's Reynolds's moving account of his struggle through cancer surgery, recovery, and beyond. What Reynolds has to say there is too rich to be condensed, but it's fair to say that one of the most important insights of the book, and the insight that lends to the book's title, is that Reynolds experienced his illness as an invitation to a whole new life.

Reynolds tells how he denied the existence of his cancer, how he was filled with anger and resentment when he realized that he was very sick, and how he struggled in the painful months after his debilitating but life-saving surgery. Here was a once robust, active man, at the prime of his life, the peak of his career, reduced to life in a wheelchair.

But Reynolds depicts his path back as a dawning realization that, in his words, "The old Reynolds has died."[26] His old self was gone. So many of the aspects of his former existence that he loved were gone. He could not get them back. Now he was faced with a choice: he could spend the rest of his life in grief for what he had lost, pitifully attempting to salvage bits and pieces and cobble a life together from the leftovers, or he could begin "a whole new life."

Reynolds chose the latter. He began again. He started over. It was not the life he might have chosen, if he were doing the choosing, but it was a good life, a life worth living. He now enjoys his greatest period of artistic productivity, turning out more novels, plays, and poems than ever.

"Find your way to be somebody else," he advises, "the next viable you—a stripped-down whole other clear-eyed person, realistic as a sawed-off shotgun and thankful for air, not to speak of the human kindness you'll meet if you get normal luck."[27]

Retirement is rarely as traumatic as spinal cancer. Yet I do think there are analogies to be made. From what I've observed, the people who fail miserably at the challenges of the later years are those who are unable to see retirement as a definite transition from one plane of existence to another. They attempt to salvage too much of their former life and drag that along with them into their next life.

I'm haunted by what a woman told me of her mother. Her mother had worked at minimum wage in a garment factory for over forty years. When she retired, her children thought she would be thrilled. She was miserable. She cried. She hung around at the gate of the factory many mornings, vainly hoping they would call her back to work. She even took an assumed name and tried to get hired, representing herself as another person.

That won't work. Your old life goes on without you. They somehow get by down at the office without your services. The school doesn't fall apart after your last day in the classroom.

You can't get the old life back. You need to lay hold of a whole new life. I think those of us who are moving toward retirement (and isn't that just about everyone here?) could do much more to prepare ourselves to make that transition to a whole new life. If our only life is our work, we are in big trouble unless we can find some new life after work. For Christians, to be retired is not to be unemployed or out of work. We can retire from being a paving contractor or a dishwasher, but we can't retire from discipleship. Churches could do a better job of helping our members to prepare themselves and to support one another during the transition into retirement.

My mother taught school twelve months a year. She had time to participate in church only on Sunday mornings. While some of

Sometimes critics of ageism replace stereotypes of the elderly as brittle, conservative, detached, senile, poor, and sick with currently popular (and equally false) stereotypes—older couples jumping out of airplanes or bouncing along zip lines. These positive stereotypes too easily privilege the affluent elderly over the impoverished elderly and tend to deny the realities of aging. They come with an incipient demand that all aging people be robust, sexually active, vigorous, self-reliant, and frenetically recreational—that is, old people should be young. The health of the young is handed to the old as an assignment, a fantasy of the good life they must strive to make reality. The aging must surf the web and submit to experts (like Dr. Northrup), must become active participants in refusing to age, should regard aging as their worst enemy, or must buy their way into elegant retirement settings that confirm their breathless pursuit of an "active lifestyle." Grim pessimism gives way to an unrealistic optimism that fails to see elderhood as a God-given form of life with its own trials and benefits.[8]

Because we live in a scientific, mechanistic culture, there is a tendency to view aging as a problem to be solved or as a plea for better social policy. Therefore, we focus on questions of when and how older people ought to move out of the labor pool and how we can avoid poverty, prevent disease, and work the health care system to our advantage.

While Christianity is an incarnational faith—physical and fiscal concerns are valid—the Christian faith has more interests than the merely material. Framing discussions of old age in a simply naturalistic way testifies to our lack of scriptural imagination. One of the gifts of the church is to stoke, fund, and fuel our imaginations. In approaching aging as an exclusively materialistic or social policy problem to be solved, we separate chronological aging from any larger story within which to make sense of elderhood and become sidetracked by debates over means without thoughtful consideration of ultimate ends. As Christians we have a grander narrative that fits our aging lives into an account that's larger than ourselves and sets our little selves within the pageant of God's vocation for us and God's salvation of the world.

Into Aging with a Truthful Story

Arthur Frank says that our imaginations are gripped by a myth that determines our views of health care: "I was in health yesterday. Today I am temporarily sick, but after medical intervention, tomorrow I'll be healthy once again."[9] Aging rebukes this myth. Not everyone who is ill gets well; aging often comes with chronic pain and illnesses. Then there's the problem of death's inevitability.

Here's a more truthful account of health: everyone who is well today can count on being sick sometime in the future, and anyone who recovers from an illness will, sooner or later, have more illness and probably more pain, and, even if they don't, everyone dies. Because many of the physically debilitating aspects of aging cannot be "fixed," the "I was in health, then I got sick, but tomorrow I'll be fixed and healthy again" story is a fantasy that plays into our self-deceit about the omnipotence of modern science and medicine. Aging is not an illness, a tragedy, or a problem awaiting a solution; aging is the price we pay for life, which is a greater gift than we deserve.

Poet A. R. Ammons, reflecting on aging, admits, "The people of my time are passing away . . . well, we never thought we would live forever (although we did) and now it looks like we won't."[10] So if we can't live forever, what is our story?

The Christian faith is based on a story more truthful than the fairy tales of the world. We Christians claim that the scriptural narrative of the death and resurrection of Jesus Christ gives us a means for making sense of our lives. Rather than the "I was in health, then I got sick, but tomorrow I'll be fixed and healthy again" fantasy, Christians learn a story that goes something like this:

> God gave me the precious gift of life. My life is on loan from God. Even more valuable than my life, God in Christ called me, gave me a vocation to discipleship, whereby my life is caught up in the purposes of God and I am utilized by God in God's salvation of humanity. I am not a god or an immortal angel; I am a finite being, an animal who is subject to the limitations of being a creature who is not the Creator. My life is not my own. I live on borrowed breath. The eternal significance and sustenance of my life is up to God and not to me. While I have life, in whatever physical or mental condition I find myself, in

whatever circumstances I am cast, I am called to glorify, to serve, and to enjoy God and God's good gifts and to use whatever gifts God has given me in service to the needs of others. Eventually God will take back the life with which God has entrusted me so that I might be given the gift of glorifying and enjoying God forever.

Loss

No matter how good the stories we live by are, we haven't told the truth about aging without speaking of loss as an undeniable, persistent aspect of aging—"sans teeth, sans eyes, sans taste, sans everything." While losses can be experienced throughout life, they greatly accumulate during our last years. We outlive friends, we are the only surviving sibling, we are forced to move from beloved, predictable places, and we run out of time to accomplish all that we would like to undertake.

Donald Hall tells the truth when he writes, "To grow old is to lose everything."[11] While visiting parishioners in a nursing home, I asked a ninety-two-year-old woman if she would like to have prayer before I left her room. "No," she said. "I'm mad at God. God's taken everything from me but won't take me."

"If only I could walk once more in the street in front of my house in Greenville," sighed another nursing home resident that same day.

By evening, in my study, even I said to myself, "I'm going to run out of Sundays before I do justice to all the Scripture that ought to be preached."

Some losses are necessary in order for us to enter the second half of life with confidence. "We cannot live the afternoon of life according to the program of life's morning," said Carl Jung, "for what was great in the morning will be little at evening, and what in morning was true will at evening have become a lie."[12]

Loss is the risk we take, and sometimes the price we pay, for loving. Loss and loneliness are the twin fruits of love. Losses accumulate, social engagements and supportive people fall by the wayside, the world passes by, and we feel deserted. Most of the downsizing we experience in aging is involuntary, making our losses even more difficult to bear. Friends depart. Familiar landmarks disappear. If a spouse or partner dies, we fear it might be said of us, "She died from a broken heart."

Yet suffering loss can reposition us to receive something else. I have seen widows move from deep grief over the death of a husband to renewed self-worth.

"Who knows? Maybe now I'm more me than my old married me," a woman said a year after her husband's death.

As we learned when we downsized and moved into a much smaller home in our sixties, some losses can be unburdening, joyfully letting go of superfluous accumulation. Forgiveness is a kind of loss, but many Christians testify that such faithful loss can be joyful release.

The presence of others who continue to love and care for us, even in our loss, is of inestimable value in helping us to live through our assorted bereavements and, to some degree, to reintegrate and go on. God has made us for relationship, and the pain of the loss of relationships is often best assuaged by other relationships. When someone says, "We joined this church because everyone here was so warm and friendly," that's not an inappropriate reason for church.

In delivering Meals on Wheels, one quickly discovers it's not the meal but the visit that brings the recipient the most nourishment.

Because the major narrative of aging involves loss and decline, this narrative can stifle our determination to see opportunities as we age. Aging, and our bleak stories about it, may be a source of the storied midlife crisis. No wonder some have a disorienting crisis at midlife when they're being told that they are now moving inexorably toward the worst time of their lives.[13] Judging from research into people's reports of happiness, it's more difficult to be forty than to be seventy, perhaps because of the looming grim prospect of aging. Surprisingly, reported life satisfaction actually begins to rise after fifty. It's easier to attend your fiftieth college reunion than your twentieth.

Amid the losses attendant upon aging, we have to find a way to, in effect, write a new chapter in our biography. Speaking more theologically, we must embrace the story that God is writing with our lives, learning to love the plot that is taking an unexpected or even undesired turn. Gerontologist James Woodward says that a key to negotiating the realities of aging is to move from an impossible desire for liberation *from* old age (Dr. Northrup and her ageless goddess) to a joyful embrace of the liberation *of* old age (the Nightblooming Jazzmen).[14] While there are losses in aging, finding a special sort of freedom is possible. We can be liberated from fantasies of eternal usefulness and indispensability to the world and from the misconception of the impossibility of a meaningful last stage in life. Old age can be received as a gift of freedom from an overly self-conscious youth or the rigorous constraints and responsibilities of middle age.

Can we, by faith, come to say, "The LORD gave, and the LORD has taken away; blessed be the name of the LORD" (Job 1:21 NRSV)? Can the Christian faith and its master story give us the means of narrating our lives as, "The Lord gave me one sort of life, but living a long life has meant that much of my earlier life has been taken away, so now the Lord is giving me a new life"?

Aging Bodies

The human body grows up, degenerates, and declines. Aging entails predictable bodily constraints. Research indicates that the brains of healthy older adults continue to work well but more slowly; our brains do not process information as swiftly, and our reflection time increases. These changes in brain functioning may account for why it seems as if time moves faster while we are moving slower. There is also a documentable loss of flexibility in solving problems and thinking about alternatives—aging negatively affects the brain's ability to modify approaches to problems or to easily adapt to unexpected changes in life—and a reduced capacity for multitasking. Most of us older adults note that we have slower recovery from physical or mental exertion and from surgery or illness. We more quickly and more frequently sense fatigue. Yet slower brain functioning does not mean mental incapacity.

In spite of decreased adaptability in problem solving, we aged can take heart that it is possible to teach an old dog new tricks because successful aging requires behavioral change. Aging bodies offer us the possibility to correct our disembodied, docetic theologies and to embrace the embodied, incarnational nature of the Christian faith. A refusal to disparage or to deny physical realities or to paper them over with superficial gnostic sentimentality is a gift of the theology of incarnation. Because God Almighty took on our aging flesh, we can joyfully adapt to bodily, fleshly limits as well.

You don't have to be an adaptive, innovative person at heart to age successfully, but it helps. As someone cheerfully told me after her mobility and independence were ended following a bad fall, "I am now adapting to a revised lifestyle."

Among the physiological changes of aging are a decrease in cellular water content along with an increase in fat cells in relation to muscle cells, leading to less muscle mass and decreased elasticity; a reduction in bone mass and minerals, making bones more brittle and raising the risk of fractures; and deterioration in the range, flexibility, and composition of surfaces and joints, increasing the likelihood of inflammation, fractures, and arthritis.[15] Changes in the cardiovascular system greatly impact the health of some older adults. These biological changes account for a sense of diminishment in physical abilities among the aging, but they also mean that even modest physical activity has great benefit for the aging body.

"Have you had a fall in the last three months?" has become the standard first question put to me at the beginning of any medical exam, even a dermatological checkup. Falls are the leading cause of fatal and nonfatal injuries in older adults. More than eight hundred thousand older adults are hospitalized each year due to injuries from falls. Mortality rates from fall-related injuries are estimated to be as high as 20 to 30 percent. Fear of falling is a significant cause of older adult inactivity.[16]

In speaking of the physical, bodily aspects of aging, we are not veering from our goal of thinking like Christians. In Christ, God became embodied in our always aging human flesh. Jesus Christ experienced our fleshly suffering and temptations in every way (Heb. 4:15) with a notable exception—the sufferings and temptations attendant with life after thirty-three.

Should we regard the physiological changes in our aging bodies as restraints and disabilities, or should we see them as predictable aspects of being over sixty-five? James Woodward finds it interesting that when asked, "How is your health?" the majority of older adults judge themselves to be "healthy," even though they are often less healthy than at any other time in their lives. Perhaps these adults have successfully expanded and adapted their notions of health. They have learned that a decline in physical abilities is not necessarily connected to a decline in other abilities, that decline is not synonymous with cessation.

"I can still go anywhere I really need or want to go," quipped a septuagenarian as he hobbled up the church steps, "with the exception of Mount Everest."

Concepts like health and wellness are complex, multidimensional, and sometimes even contradictory. "Good health" looks different for different people. Sometimes our notions of wellness are merely a commentary on the wiles of life in a consumerist society that tells us it's possible to buy our way into a life worth living. Woodward says that it's futile to attempt to deny or fend off old age, to defy the inevitable changes in identity that aging entails. However, he also believes that we can come to a place where we can embrace physical changes as part of who we are.[17] Can God give us the grace to see our aging bodies and minds not as cruel biological fate but as God-ordained ways of being human?

We aging can take heart that medical research indicates that physical decline related to aging may not be as steep as we once thought and that a number of measures can be taken to minimalize or at least delay debility. These steps can be beneficial in slowing the deleterious effects of bodily aging: calorie reduction (fewer calories for the body to process), exercise (any is better than none), a nontoxic environment (eliminate smoking, alcohol, and a fall-prone setting), management of stress, and ingestion of more fruits and green vegetables and less meat, salt, and sugar.

Older adults are wise to be suspicious of some of the (seemingly monthly) announcements of dramatic benefits to be had through various dietary measures. There is no conclusive scientific evidence of the benefits of antioxidants. While celiac disease is a serious disorder, many who do not have celiac disease believe that restricting gluten makes them feel better, though there is little scientific evidence for other conditions of gluten intolerance. The placebo effect is real. If eating kale makes you feel better, by all means, eat kale.

Remember Geritol? There is no scientific evidence that it helps those who drink it daily, and yet thousands continue to believe it helps.

As far back as the 1930s, a rat study found that rats who were fed half of the calories fed to other rats did better in all aspects of aging (except for wound healing and viruses). Many researchers believe that a reduction in calorie intake is the single most important factor in extending longevity in laboratory animals, but few physicians believe it's a realistic strategy for humans.[18] We'll never know if dietary restriction dramatically helps human aging—humans lack the willpower for a dramatic, voluntary reduction of calories, and as Scripture teaches (Gen. 3:6), we tend to succumb to food temptations. The best advice seems to be that for all post-middle-age adults, fewer calories, achieved through eating less or brief bouts of fasting, is a good idea.

Normal, predictable aging will not be defied. The internet is full of wild but scientifically unsubstantiated assertions of the discovery of *the* nutritional key to halting the ravages of time. Aging cannot be defeated, only somewhat resisted, so it is wise to beware of exaggerated claims regarding the benefits of super foods.

Exercise positively impacts senior bodies and minds, but it is not magic. Regular, sensible exercise does not seem to affect longevity but does improve the quality of life in the aged. Physical debility is accelerated by disuse of our bodies. Exercise can't control or stop aging; however, exercise can lessen the slope and the speed of physical and mental decline.

The goal in regard to diet and exercise should not be an increase in longevity but rather an augmentation of healthy years and a concomitant decrease in sick years. Sickness is a more significant factor in longevity even than exercise. If we cured cancer, we could add three to four years to Americans' longevity; a heart disease cure would win us an additional six to seven years. Here's an incentive for longevity: people who live past ninety tend to consume fewer health resources, go into nursing care only at the very end of their lives, and depart quickly.[19]

Stress can have negative health consequences for the aged, but a lack of all stress, leading to social, physical, and mental inactivity, can be deleterious. Relieving the aged of all sources of stress isn't wise, particularly the stress that is induced through normal interaction with others. Stress—if rightly managed and seen as encouragement to keep moving, to keep contributing, and to keep relating to others—can be beneficial.

"Having to raise my two grandchildren, even when I'm sixty, has added a decade to my life, whether I wanted it or not," said a grandmother recently. She may be right.

You've perhaps heard of some of the interesting research on brain plasticity, the way the brain develops and responds to changing contexts and demands placed on it. It's important to note that brain studies show that brain development can continue into old age.[20] But this does not occur without stimulation. Beneficial stimulation is more than playing brain-training games, which have yet to show much positive effect. The best brain stimulation comes from having connections with and responsibilities for others, as does the grandmother whose brain is forced to help her raise her two grandchildren—whether she wanted to or not—or the church members who must, "Be tolerant with each other and, if someone has a complaint against anyone, forgive each other. As the Lord forgave you, so also forgive each other" (Col. 3:13), whether they want to or not.

Woodward closes his book with practical advice on how to achieve successful aging: learn something new, take the opportunity to be someone different, prepare for death.[21]

Do you note anything missing from Woodward's steps to successful aging? God.

For Christians, the major goad to successful aging is active discipleship, fulfillment of our vocation, service, and Sabbath-like connection with God. The church shouldn't be in the business of promoting excessive self-concern; that is well stoked in this culture without help from the church. Instead, the church should neither excuse anyone from active witness to the faith nor treat the normal aches and pains of aging as if they were an injustice or a form of martyrdom.

The church must teach people of all ages to see older adults as a God-given resource.[22] For the young who have not experienced the joy of taking responsibility for the needs of anyone else, caring for the aged can be an aspect of God's vocation. For the aging, an increase of years can be seen as an opportunity God offers us to enjoy some of life's blessings that we may earlier have neglected, an occasion for us to witness to all God's people that Jesus Christ can be faithfully served in any season of life, even in a time replete with physical decline, pain, and ill health.

Gray hair is often seen as a sign of wisdom. I once read a story about a young actor who was asked why she wanted to be in a film directed by a ninety-year-old. She replied with something like, "Clint Eastwood's wrinkles and weathered face show how much life has taught him."

Studies of aging highlight the importance of cultivating a positive frame of mind. Of course, positive thinking cannot compensate for the ill effects of poverty, pain, or poor physical or mental health in old age. That's one of my misgivings about Richard Rohr's popular *Falling Upward*. Rohr's cheerful self-help book on aging makes successful aging mostly a matter of an upbeat mental attitude. He thus panders to a desire for personal control. "No one can keep you from the second half of your own life but yourself. Nothing can inhibit your second journey except your own lack of courage, patience, and lack of imagination. Your second journey is all yours to walk or to avoid."[23] Norman Vincent Peale *redivivus*.

Telling myself the lie that I'm a seventy-year-old with a twenty-five-year-old body and brain, far from helping me negotiate the challenges of aging, makes me feel as if any of my discomfort with aging is my own fault, a failure to achieve a positive attitude.

An exclusively affirmative depiction of aging, with praise for the energetic and good-humored elderly as exemplars of successful aging, ought to be chastened by admission that a blissful old age is often dependent on material and situational factors for which the cheerful elderly can take little credit and that are not enjoyed by the majority of their aging cohort. For a Christian to be too cheerful about life may be evidence of a disregard for the plight of those who have not been blessed with health and wealth.[24]

For those who would like a less moralistic, more realistic take on life's "second journey," I commend Mary Sarton's powerful though bleak little novel, *As We Are Now*. Sarton's character Caroline Spencer, who at seventy-six is consigned by her family to a "home," rages like Lear that she is in nothing more than a concentration camp for the old.[25] Caroline speaks of aging as a journey that is like visiting a strange, unknown land that isn't understood until one gets there.

Rohr's talk of the second journey being all ours to walk or to avoid is the message that we independent, affluent, control-loving, privileged persons love to hear. We enjoy thinking of ourselves as capable of overcoming all life's obstacles by our sheer grit, overlooking how much of our agency and independence has been given to us through our economic, educational, and social privileges rather than through our personal virtues. As Christians, we are who we are in part as a gift of God. We are God's people. The church is curiously missing from Rohr's book.

Rohr paints a rosy picture of the second half of life as a serene time when we wise and magnanimous people allow our basic goodness to flourish, leaving behind those sour elderly who have a bad attitude. He speaks of the second half of life (a phrase he picked up from Jung) as the "crowning" time of life, a summit from which we look down with charity and magnanimity on all with a bright, luminous gaze. It's easier to think of old age as the crowning time of life if one is not completely dependent on the beneficence of the Social Security system.

Yet in fairness to Rohr's positive thinking, much evidence shows that even people with physical and financial disabilities can be helped by the cultivation of a positive general disposition. A key factor in happiness is having a modicum of control over one's life and some sense of independence and agency. Though we don't have complete control over our finances or our health, we do have some modicum of management of our attitude. If Rohr is right that frame of mind and general disposition can make a difference in how we go through aging, then the church—a place where our imaginations are stoked and funded and where our inclinations and desires are formed, reformed, and cultivated—surely has a role to play, which must be the reason why Rohr's work is so widely embraced by my own church.

The Grant Study

In 1947 researchers began the Grant Study by studying men who graduated from Harvard in 1948. (Only men were at Harvard then.) Then researchers returned to these subjects throughout the course of their lives and thereby produced our most thorough and important longitudinal study of college-educated men. George Vaillant, a widely published Dartmouth psychiatrist, mined the data from the research and interviewed the subjects of the Grant Study who were still living— men now in their eighties—to uncover the factors associated with successful male aging.[26]

Vaillant defines the goal of successful aging this way: "To . . . retain human dignity despite the ravages of mortality."[27] As Vaillant notes, while this is a task for anyone who faces imminent death, the successfully aging demonstrate that mortal life can be good, right to the very end.

The Grant Study shows that long marriages are good for emotional well-being in the last decades of life. Through marriage, Vaillant theorizes, some of our inherent narcissism is overcome with empathy and love and our defense mechanisms and social intelligence improve. Perhaps this validates the church's claim that the best way to love one another is by making and keeping promises "for better, for worse, for richer, for poorer, in sickness and in health" in youth or in old age.

Alcoholism is a major detriment to aging bodies, says the Grant Study, suggesting that the virtue of temperance has a biological benefit.

The Grant Study notes not only stability but also surprising change in our personalities as we age. The course of life shapes the self, and the self shapes life's course. Coping mechanisms enable the aging to adapt their thinking and feeling in beneficial ways. Old habits and patterns of relating to others can be modified. A very ambitious and demanding person may in later life become more serene and reflective. A relatively solitary individual may at last have the time and the inclination to venture forth into community.

While King Lear reminds us that real personality change is rare in people of any age, the men of the Grant Study show that some aging people change their disposition to better align themselves with their changed circumstances. Sometimes they change because they want to stay connected with the norms among younger cohorts. They modify their life patterns to fit in with contemporary lifestyles in order to maintain links with their children and grandchildren. Vaillant asserts that changing interaction patterns with younger cohorts can be a major influence on older people. That's another reason why it is good to be in the church: churches provide the most significant multigenerational interaction opportunities for many of us.

Sometimes aging gives us the freedom to express aspects of our personality that were repressed or set aside because of certain life demands and family responsibilities. The mother who always presented an exemplary, official demeanor to her children may become more accommodating and fun loving in old age. The father who was always away and on the road with his job now has time to be the perfect elementary school volunteer. Adaptability, flexibility, and creativity are not only required to have a successful last quarter of life but also necessary for those who aspire to serve and worship a living God.

Affluence aids successful aging. The Grant Study found marked differences in the last decades of life for the comparatively rich and the relatively poor. The rich live longer than the poor, free of concern about getting by from one day to the next. Queen Elizabeth's long life may be more attributable to her royal financial holdings than to her prudent lifestyle.

Successful aging is linked to intellectual curiosity and growth. Ruel Howe quipped that you don't grow old, rather "when you cease to grow, you are old."[28] A paradox of aging is that, while there is physical decline and multiple loss of abilities, the last decades of life can bring more social engagement and more extensive intellectual interest. Programs such as Road Scholar and OLLI (Osher Lifelong Learning Institute) show that seniors are an expanding, eager market for travel and lifelong learning experiences. Ironically, we older people who are short on future life often have more time for growth and study as well as a greater sense of urgency. "If I'm going to learn more about opera, I need to get started now," said my wife, Patsy, at seventy.

Education is an important factor in aging, not so much because of what is learned, says Vaillant, but because the achievement of a high degree of education demonstrates traits of perseverance and goal setting. Reading interest and fluency contribute to successful aging.[29] A higher education level also adds to positive personal regard.

Politically, liberals negotiate the challenges of aging better than political conservatives, Vaillant claims, because liberals are more likely to be open to new ideas and to approve of the younger generation's behavior. In the Grant Study, liberals tended to have had highly educated mothers and to have gone to graduate school. They displayed creativity and used sublimation as a defense (diverting an instinctual activity, such as sex, into a higher and more socially productive activity, such as education). While conservatives are cautious of novelty, they make more money, play more sports, and are twice as likely to be religious as liberals, all of which can aid aging.[30]

Vaillant was surprised by factors that were not as important as we might think. Ancestral longevity and genetic inheritance are not as important as popular wisdom suggests ("Choose your parents wisely"). Psychosomatic distress earlier in life neither contributes to nor deters longevity.[31] A high cholesterol count doesn't seem to be important. Even a bleak childhood is not a significant factor in successful aging, according to Vaillant.[32]

Here are the eight factors that *did* predict healthy aging: not being a smoker or stopping smoking while young; an adaptive, coping personality (poor Lear); mature defenses; an absence of alcohol abuse; a healthy weight; a stable marriage; some exercise; and the acquisition of some years of higher education. Vaillant also stresses agency: "Whether we live to a vigorous old age lies not so much in our stars or our genes as in ourselves," a thought that echoes Rohr.[33]

There is an increasing awareness, stimulated by research like the Grant Study, that social factors may be as important for successful aging as physical factors. Stimulation provided by the psychosocial environment has beneficial effects on the elderly. Connection with younger cohorts is important. It is never too soon and never too late to begin the physical, intellectual, and socially connective work required for successful aging.

Aging Out of Control

Throughout Vaillant's work is his recognition, based on the Grant Study, that one of the challenges associated with aging is having to cope with having so much of life out of our control. No matter how hard we try, how careful our eating habits, or how much we study, much of our lives is already determined genetically, physically, and emotionally, a truth that is particularly unpleasant for Americans who like to think of their lives as personal projects, self-constructions.

From what I have experienced, loss of control due to aging is a greater challenge if a person has (1) been a pastor whose parishioners' affection and friendship were freely offered, (2) been a bishop whose authority and power were bestowed rather than earned, (3) been a writer whose work schedule was at his own discretion, (4) enjoyed good physical and mental health throughout his life, and (5) always had enough money to buy everything he needed and much that he wanted.

Though Vaillant gives short shrift to the role of religion in successful aging, I see a potentially positive effect of the Christian faith on older folks who feel they are losing control over their lives. Think of the Christian life as training in having our lives out of our control. Our lives are not our own. We don't have to self-concoct the significance of our selves. Who we are, what we ought to do, and what we mean are God-given gifts, not personal attainments. There is freedom in answering "What is the significance of the life I've lived?" with "God only knows."

The typical losses of aging, the sense of being out of control, give us the opportunity to recollect Jesus's curious statement that we cannot enter God's realm unless we "turn [our] lives around and become like this little child" (Matt. 18:3). Many of the aging learn that turning back toward the vulnerability and neediness of childhood is not something that we decide; it is what life does to us. Everyone who lives long enough looks small, vulnerable, and out of control someday. That's no fun, but in the words of Jesus, our reduction and diminution place us in range of the kingdom.

Is it any wonder that some older adults attempt to take matters in hand and self-terminate or direct someone else to terminate them?

In his letter to the elderly, Pope John Paul II tackled the issue of euthanasia. The pope lamented that

> in recent years the idea of euthanasia has lost for many people the sense of horror which it naturally awakens in those who have a sense of respect for life. Certainly it can happen that, when grave illness involves unbearable suffering, the sick are tempted to despair and

their loved ones or those responsible for their care feel compelled by
a misguided compassion to consider the solution of "an easy death"
as something reasonable. Here it should be kept in mind that the
moral law allows the rejection of "aggressive medical treatment"[34] and
makes obligatory only those forms of treatment which fall within the
normal requirements of medical care, which in the case of terminal
illness seeks primarily to alleviate pain. But euthanasia, understood as
directly causing death, . . . regardless of intentions and circumstances,
. . . is always an intrinsically evil act, a violation of God's law and an
offence against the dignity of the human person.[35]

Though I'm not so sure that euthanasiasts should be judged so
harshly, it's true that euthanasia can play on the deceit that we are
in charge, that our lives are our possessions to use as we will. The
irony, of course, is that dying is about as out of control as life can
get. Is it in our hands to judge when our lives are no longer worth
living and when our continued living is without meaning to others?
Are we given mastery over how our lives end? The same could be said
about end-of-life directives, meticulous preplanning of funerals, and
the distribution of our legacies. While these practices can be evidence
of a healthy confrontation with our mortality, in what ways do they
give us the illusion of control precisely at the time when we are totally
out of control? Remember Lear!

Nevertheless, as Thomas Moore puts it, "Aging is an activity. It
is something you do, not something that happens. When you age—
active verb—you are proactive. If you really age, you become a better
person. If you simply grow old passively, you get worse. . . . You will
be unhappy as you continue the fruitless fight against time."[36]

Vaillant highlights the ways that mature defenses are an intelligent,
creative way to exercise agency in our lives in spite of our loss of
control. Altruism, anticipation, humor, sublimation, and suppression
of negative feelings make strong, positive contributions to successful
aging. (Vaillant previously wrote a fine book on the importance of
coping mechanisms, The Wisdom of the Ego.[37]) These defenses help
increase our resilience and ability to negotiate life's challenges without propagating the myth that we are in control. Though we can't
control the trials that come our way, we can choose our responses to
the contests presented by our aging.

Regret

The poet T. S. Eliot lists three ills of aging: ills of the body, ills of the world, and ills of the past when one is apt to feel "the rending pain of re-enactment of all that you've done, . . . of things ill done and done to others' harm."[38]

Some older persons are consumed with remorse due to life paths taken and not taken, fractured relationships, and regrettable life choices. Dealing with regret requires deciding how to think about things that shouldn't have been done or should have happened but didn't. The intensity of sorrow is often dependent on the distance between what we would have preferred to have happened in life and what actually happened.

Sometimes the best cure for regret is to introduce ambivalence toward what we would have preferred. The prized achievement that we thought we simply had to obtain can be reframed, viewed in a way that enables us to see that the coveted goal was not so worthy anyway. This introduction of ambivalence acts as a counterweight to the backward, downward tug of regret.

Still, for Christians, the gift God gives us for dealing with regret and remorse is more than the cultivation of ambivalence toward the mistakes we've made. Nearly every Sunday the pastor invites us to "confess our sin to Almighty God," an invitation for everyone to un-burden and leave their regrets at the altar. Jesus commanded us to forgive our enemies, and sometimes our greatest enemy is our vain attempt to live our lives without mistakes and failures.

Learning to Love the Life God Gives

I believe that a fundamental secret of successful aging is learning to affirm the lives God gives us in the face of regret that God didn't give us the lives we thought we needed to live happily. As Rabbi Abraham Heschel put it, aging "is not a defeat but a victory, not a punishment but a privilege."[39]

If you are a goal-oriented person, you are accustomed to post-poning joy and satisfaction into the future. But then you wake up one day and discover that your future is shrinking. More yesterdays than tomorrows. Successful aging requires finding a way to love our lives today, regardless of whether or not our cherished goals were reached or valued relationships were maintained. Excessive investment in specific life projects can be a setup for sadness. Therefore, many of us must find joy in noninstrumental, goal-less experiences. The pleasure of travel or attendance at parties and athletic events is that they have no higher purpose, no goal other than sheer, gratuitous, momentary, pointless joy.

Aging gives those of us who have goal-oriented, telic personalities the opportunity to become contemplatives. Brilliant John Stuart Mill was a precocious child (he allegedly mastered Greek by age three). In his late twenties, Mill had a nervous breakdown and was forced to find activities unrelated to his ambition. Mill asked himself, "Would achievement of my ambitions make me happy?" He decided that reaching his goals would not lead to contentment. Mill stopped allowing his goals to determine the value of his life and began living in the moment and enjoying himself and the life he had.[40]

In our last decades of life we realize that we are going to miss out on the realization of some of our aspirations and may have to relinquish some of the things we most enjoy. Still, this time in life can be not only a time of simplification and limitation but also a period in which our scope of interests expands and we are given opportunities that we have been previously unable to enjoy. In focusing on the essentials, are we going back to basics or are we moving forward to whom God always wanted us to be? With the freedom given in retirement, some pursue completion of their bucket list. As T. S. Eliot said, "Old men ought to be explorers."[41]

Simplicity can become the elderly's chief virtue. Our lives are often in turmoil because we're busy striving to create, to assemble, and to accumulate. In old age, complex lives can whittle down to the basics; we are free to reclaim the essentials. William May, in his book *The Patient's Ordeal*, says that ritual—a love of the predictable and the familiar—often characterizes the lives of the elderly "not merely because memory lapses into the familiar, repetitive grooves, but because the Pilgrim has at long last, learned to travel light . . . to live by simple truths and simple gifts."[42] The prophet Micah describes the person who focuses on the basics:

> He has told you, O mortal, what is good;
>   and what does the LORD require of you
> but to do justice, and to love kindness,
>   and to walk humbly with your God? (6:8 NRSV)

After a guest speaker at our church extolled the joys of divesting ourselves of some of our superfluous material goods and living a simpler lifestyle, one of our older members testified, "I've spent most of my adult life accumulating stuff, collecting, buying, and getting. Then the Lord saw fit to take it away from me, and my life got radically simplified. Now, as I enjoy my little room at the retirement center, I'm surprised by how good it feels. Makes me wonder if this was the simpler life God intended for me all along."

Reflecting on his loss of sexual desire, Sophocles said he felt "like a slave escaped from a cruel master."[43] Aging, when viewed as more than physiological deterioration, can be seen as a peculiar freedom. Sexual desire that jerked us around for so much of our lives may be quelled as we age. We can also find ourselves free of our lust for social status, along with anxieties over prestige or fame, as our drive to impress others or to make a name for ourselves weakens. Free of the weight of many of our adult responsibilities, we may view aging as life's last great adventure and develop a capacity for playfulness. While there's not much research on the benefits of playfulness, what does exist indicates that "playfulness in later life improves cognitive, emotional, social and psychological functioning and healthy aging."[44] At last there's time to devote to a cherished hobby in which we lose ourselves, free of excessive self-concern or the need to be productive. Time to join the Red Hat Society and make up for the sobriety of youth.

"In our first marriages," explained a couple of octogenarians during our premarital counseling session, "we married for love with responsibilities. Now we get to marry just for love."

"Your relationship surpasses even the irresponsible goofiness of teenage love," I said to them. "It's wonderful!"

The Godfather (part 1) ends with the brutal Mafia don, played by Marlon Brando, happily playing games in the garden with his little grandson. Though Don Corleone lived badly, scoundrel though he was, he got a contented dying anyway. As writer Tom Robbins put it, "Never too late for a happy childhood."[45]

The twelfth-century Chinese poet Lu Yu, in his poem "Written in a Carefree Mood," speaks about old age as the recovery of the child within. He describes how a nearly seventy-year-old can act just like he did as a boy: he heads to school with a "battered book" under his arm, "whooping with delight when he spies some mountain fruits."[46]

In his memoir, *The Summing Up* (written at age sixty-four!), Somerset Maugham noted that old age frees us of certain passions that caused mischief in earlier life. "Old age has its pleasures, which, though different, are not less than the pleasures of youth."[47] Mary Pipher says that "the old like verbal and physical affection and, unlike the young, are under no illusion that they do not need love."[48]

Delight can be a companion as we rejoice when younger friends move into positions where they can make special contributions and flourish. We've given them a helping hand up and now can relish our protégés' accomplishments. Fewer cares and responsibilities weigh us down, so we at last have time to stop and smell the roses. Relatively trivial things can be acknowledged for their triviality as we are given world enough and time to focus on matters of greater importance. Stripped of our own ambitions, we more fully delight in the achievements of others. Gratitude, which may have been in short supply in earlier stages of life, now blossoms in us, and we say with the psalmist,

> the boundary lines have fallen for me in pleasant places;
> I have a goodly heritage. (Ps. 16:6 NRSV)

Empathy is another reward of old age. Looking back, we see that life can be tough for everybody. That's why the aged are often more generous, less severe in their judgments, less envious, kinder, and more compassionate than the young. Age gives perspective on the ups and downs of life. We take the long view. Pondering our own struggles to grow up, to become established in our marriage or job, we may have greater sympathy for the struggles of the young. Having enjoyed the benefits of good health, we may be given particular sensitivity for younger people stressed by ill health.

"As a young man, just starting out, I went hungry for nearly a month," said an older man to me after service one Sunday. "I swore to God I would do my part to feed others when I got the chance. Don't turn away anybody from our church door who says they're hungry. You give them what they need; I'll gladly repay."

When my late friend and writer Reynolds Price heard that President Clinton could be impeached for his wrongdoing, Reynolds sent a note of consolation: "Dear Mr. President: I've done worse. Reynolds."

Toward the end of his life, crusty old Malcolm Muggeridge wrote, "When I embarked I worried about having a cabin with a porthole, whether I should be asked to sit at the Captain's table with the most attractive passengers. All such considerations became pointless since I shall soon be disembarking. The world that I shall soon be leaving seems ever more beautiful. Those I love, I can love even more, since I have nothing to ask of them but their love; the passion to accumulate possessions, the need to be noticed and to be important, is so evidently absurd that it can no longer be entertained."[49]

Christians are given the capacity to be honest about life's ending. Awareness of our mortality can add value to the present time. My late friend Peter Gomes, minister of Memorial Church, Harvard, often testified to his great delight of waking up each morning and saying to himself (and to the Lord), "Well, I have awakened to another day. This day, any day really, becomes good when it is an unexpected gift. Thanks be to God."

When my friend Peter slipped away to "the undiscover'd country from whose bourn no traveller returns,"[50] I gave thanks to God that Peter's faith had enabled him to savor each of his last days as a surprising bequest.

Perhaps honesty about our mortality is fruit of a sense of God's eternity. To believe that God is in and yet beyond time, that God is eternal yet reaches out to us in our temporality, can be a comfort to older people. Looking back, we see things we should have done differently and would have done differently if we knew then what we know now. There are problems that will not be solved and mistakes that will not be righted in this life. So much is beyond repair here, now. That's when God's eternality is our consolation. We are given the long view. A Scripture-engendered sense of divine eternality may account for the irony that many aging people report that in a time of physical decline and a shrinking personal world they feel they have an increased spiritual and intellectual capacity.

As he aged, my father-in-law (Carl Parker, the same one who, in retirement, pulled a collapsible camper through Manhattan) talked a great deal about the weather. "How's the weather up there?" was his greeting when we phoned. I wonder if the elderly talk so much about the weather not because they have nothing better to talk about but because they have learned to take life one day at a time, appreciating the present, marveling at the weather, fair or foul, living in the moment, appreciating even mundane meteorology.

We enjoyed taking my mother on family trips when our children were young. Stuck in a long line at an amusement park or languishing in stalled traffic, we marveled at my mother's seemingly endless capacity to notice even the most humdrum detail of our surroundings and comment.

"What an interesting tree that is," she said as we sweltered on the freeway in Los Angeles. "It's rare to see a palm growing that straight and proud." Being on our way out of the world makes the mundane more dear.

By the grace of God we can receive gratitude for otherwise routine tasks. The person who had to rush through the preparation of meals now has time to enjoy spending an afternoon putting together a gourmet dinner for friends. A retired, high-powered business executive told me, "My greatest joy these days is serving on my church's altar guild. I who always had to be up front and in charge have now learned to cherish anonymously polishing the brassware and arranging the flowers so others can worship."

These days, when I encounter a flight of steps, I walk up them gratefully, remembering friends who are now unable to climb. If I am still able to take the stairs, I have a moral imperative to do so.

Called into Aging

For Christians, the chief freedom that comes with aging is the freedom to give ourselves more fully to our vocation, our partnership with God in God's ongoing work in the world. Having raised children and provided for a family, we are free to raise someone else's children, to provide for the needs of those who are beyond the bounds of our biological family. Having been burdened by responsibilities for our own economic well-being, we are free to assume responsibility for others, using our resources on behalf of someone whose needs are greater than our own.

Christians believe that older people are not simply a collection of bodily ills but instead are people with God-given capacities of mind and spirit, people who never outgrow accountability to God. Salvation is tied to fulfillment of vocation.

Jesus Christ, in his cross and resurrection, rearranges our definitions of "success" and "failure." The basic call to life in Christ is, in the words of the Westminster Confession of Faith, the delightfully nonutilitarian summons to "glorify God and enjoy God forever." This rather playful, noninstrumentalist vocation suggests that successful aging for Christians somehow involves rediscovering our vocation to glorify and enjoy God, in spite of everything, in the last quarter of our lives. Even as we must learn to love the body that we have, to love the friends and family that are ours, and to be grateful for this stage of life, so we must practice loving the God who has decreed that human life is bounded.

Numbering Our Days

The psalmist prays,

> So teach us to count our days
> that we may gain a wise heart. (90:12 NRSV)

The church that teaches us to count off our remaining days is the church that helps us to wise up and appreciate the days we have left, using them for no better purpose than the glorification and enjoyment of the God who will one day lovingly take back the life that God lovingly gave.

It's wisdom to know that our days are numbered. Realizing that our time is short, we do good now rather than putting it off until later.

And yet it can also be argued that fear of death breeds destructive actions that are bad for us and our neighbors. Many of our wars are fought out of fear that we or our families are in mortal danger. Fear does not bring out the best in us. When fear grips us, our worries become more narrow, and we're even more self-absorbed and suspicious of others, which may help to explain why many of the elderly are exaggeratedly self-concerned.[51]

In a *New Yorker* cartoon an old woman stands before an easel in her room, painting. She looks over her palette and peers through the little peephole in her securely locked door. The scene she paints on the canvas before her is one of chaos—bandits, brigands, and criminals charging toward her. What a worldview! The elderly have the greatest fear of being victims of violent crime and yet are the least victimized by violent crime.[52]

The philosopher Adam Smith imagines a charitable person who hears of a tragic earthquake in China. Immediately, he resolves to make a generous gift for the victims of the earthquake. But then he gets the news that disease requires the amputation of his finger. In a moment, all thoughts of others vanish and he is concerned totally with himself. Fear, pain, and illness, as intimations of mortality, tend to drive us inward.[53]

Whether numbering our days brings out the best or the worst in us is dependent in great part on whether we understand our days as gifts of God, a trust from God, a vocation to be undertaken that we may glorify God here and now so that one day we might glorify and enjoy God forever.

"Don't you know that your [aging] body is a temple of the Holy Spirit who is in you? Don't you know that [even in your last years] you have the Holy Spirit from God, and you [elderly] don't belong to yourselves? You have been bought and paid for, so honor God with your [elderly] body" (1 Cor. 6:19–20).

FIVE

With God in the Last Quarter of Life

In 1839, the American artist Thomas Cole painted a series known as *The Voyage of Life*, now displayed in a room of its own at the National Gallery in Washington, DC. In the first scene, *Childhood*, a smiling infant emerges into a lush, Edenic landscape full of potential. In *Manhood*, an adult pilots a boat on a turbulent river with swirling currents beneath and dark clouds above. Threat is all around, yet the muscular man, with hand on the tiller and eyes fixed on the river, steers the boat onward with confidence, energy, and determination.

In *Old Age*, a stooped, white-bearded old man is out on a cold winter night trudging beside the river toward where the river empties into the ocean. No life is seen, only dark clouds and a featureless ocean ahead. An angel looks down maternally on the old man, pointing him toward a golden city of lights far off in the distance. Whereas there is promise and adventure for childhood and adulthood, there is nothing for cold, exhausted old age but passive rest followed by a nebulous, distant eternity.

A major task of the contemporary church is replacement of these widely held conceptions of old age with images less pagan and more Christian. In Cole's paintings, the child, the adult, and the elder are each alone in a sometimes promising, often foreboding landscape. There is no visible human companionship and God is only hinted at by an angel. The best we can hope for, in Cole's rendition of the end of life, is a faint, solicitous angel pointing us toward a celestial realm, ethereal and indistinct.

Christians believe that the God who walks with us, who leads us onward, is in the boat with us as we drift into our last decades of life. Jesus said, "I don't call you servants any longer. . . . Instead, I call you friends" (John 15:15). In our last years, friends we have made throughout our lives can become more important than ever, including the Son of God, who calls us his friends.

Thus there is truth in theologian Eugene Bianchi's claim that "aging is more of a spiritual than a biological journey."[1]

The Importance of the Social

Though many of the challenges of aging are physical, consequences of having an aging human body, some of the most difficult changes are social and relational. The latest research on aging reveals the remarkable import of social networks, friendships, and socialization as positive contributors to successful aging. Loneliness may be more detrimental to the health of older adults than diabetes. As bad as smoking is for our health, almost as deleterious is social isolation. George Vaillant even cites studies that show that loneliness can rob us of five years of longevity.[2]

Writer Dan Buettner visited "blue zones" where people live remarkably longer. He became quite enthusiastic about eating beans, citing research that indicated that beans can be beneficial for longevity. Yet after further study of the Seventh-day Adventists in Loma Linda, California, and the residents of the Japanese island of Okinawa, Buettner decided that more important for successful aging even than diet is continuing socialization.

In America, we divide our lives into two parts: our work life and then everything else. Buettner notes that people seem to age better in societies where retirement is virtually unknown, where older men keep advising the town council on its business and older women typically care for children and do most of the cooking, thereby making essential contributions to the well-being of the family.[3]

Vaillant says that although he is a physician who is concerned about the perils of alcohol abuse, sometimes alcohol encourages socialization. "Friends are always more fun than good habits! Before and after age 50. Cultivate the richest social network you possibly can. Your life will be better for it," even if alcohol is involved.[4]

Christians live out the truth of John Wesley's dictum: "Christianity is a social religion; to turn it into a solitary affair is to destroy it."[5] Jesus gathers a group of disciples; his mission is no solo affair. Thus Christianity has always maintained that salvation is a corporate, social, group experience. Christian worship is inherently socializing—loving friends around the table. If we are to worship and serve Jesus Christ, we must do so in the company of others, making friends with those who are befriended by God. Simone Weil says that at any time in life there is nothing more salubrious for Christians than "friendship with the friends of God."[6]

God Calling Young and Old

As a child, I relished the story of the call of little Samuel when he was in service to old Eli (1 Sam. 3). God comes to the inexperienced kid, awaking him in the middle of the night with, "Samuel, Samuel . . ." rather than disturbing the sleep of the theologically trained, professional priest. At some point—say, the summer I became fifty-one—I began to resent this story. Why would God give revelation to the untrained kid that God withheld from the aging priest?

First Samuel says that the call of the prophet occurred in a dry season for spirituality. "The LORD's word was rare at that time, and visions weren't widely known" (1 Sam. 3:1). Finally, God appears—at last a vision is given—but not to the priest, old Eli, "whose eyes had grown so weak he was unable to see" (v. 2). When an epiphany occurs, it is given not to the senior citizen Eli but rather to the untrained, uncredentialed kid Samuel. He hears his name called. Samuel presumes Eli has summoned him. Eli tells the boy that he didn't call him and instructs him to go to his cot and lie down. Though Eli had been living with and working for the Lord for years, young "Samuel didn't yet know the LORD" (v. 7). A second and third time Samuel is called. "Then Eli realized that it was the LORD who was calling the boy" (v. 8). So Eli, who had years of experience with the Lord, tells Samuel, "Go and lie down. If he calls you, say, 'Speak, LORD. Your servant is listening'" (v. 9).

Though advanced in years, suffering from poor eyesight, and not the beneficiary of much recent revelation, Eli has something to contribute to this epiphany: he can help a new generation make friends with God, aiding them in interpreting their ambiguous spiritual experience as God's vocation.

The story takes an ominous turn, at least for the aging, weighted, poor-sighted priest. The Lord calls Samuel to become a prophet, a spokesperson for God, though the message that Samuel is to preach is not good news for Eli's family: "I am about to do something in Israel that will make the ears of all who hear it tingle! On that day, I will bring to pass against Eli everything I said about his household—every last bit of it! I told him that I would punish his family forever because of the wrongdoing he knew about—how his sons were cursing God, but he wouldn't stop them. Because of that I swore about Eli's household that his family's wrongdoing will never be reconciled by sacrifice or by offering" (1 Sam. 3:11–14).

God afflicts Eli for the blasphemy of his sons. If it is true, as I have heard said, "You're only as happy in retirement as your least happy child" (what is more out of your control than your child's happiness?), Eli is about to become a very unhappy older adult.

In a poignant scene, the next morning old Eli asks young Samuel what the Lord said to him. Samuel is fearful to answer, but Eli encourages him to tell him about the vision; Eli is willing to hear God's truth. So Samuel tells all. We don't know Eli's reaction to the threatening vision. We know only that little Samuel grows up and enjoys a great prophetic career in which "none of his words fall to the ground" (1 Sam. 3:19 RSV). I ask again, "Why would God bless young Samuel in ways that God did not bless faithful Eli?"

Toward the beginning of Samuel's adult ministry, the Philistines kill thousands of Israelites in a disastrous battle. Eli's ne'er-do-well sons Hophni and Phinehas had the bright idea to lug the ark of the covenant to the battle, hoping to gain magical protection for the Israelites. In the calamity that follows, the sons of Eli are killed and the victorious Philistines steal the holy ark. Poor Eli lives long enough to see his sons responsible for the loss of everything he has cherished and worked for.

A messenger is sent to Shiloh to tell the bad news to Eli, who is "sitting up on his seat by the road watching" (1 Sam. 4:13 NRSV).

Old Eli has clearly aged out of the game, sidelined from the battle, where he sits and waits in anxiety because "his heart trembled for the ark of God" (v. 13 NRSV). There's aging for you: retreat from the battle, sitting beside the road watching the world go by, disappointed and abandoned by progeny, fearfully awaiting word that everything has gone down the drain.

"Eli was 98 years old, and his eyes stared straight ahead, unable to see" (v. 15). He is told what happened. Hearing the bad news of the deaths of his sons is a blow, but when Eli is told of the fate of the ark of God, the text says, "Eli fell backward off the chair beside the gate. His neck broke, and he died because he was an old man and overweight" (v. 18). It's a sad end for the forty-year ministry of Eli.

To my mind—as an aging, formerly active, heavy priest—a chief question for us seniors who are attempting to live with and worship Eli's God is this: "Are we willing to go through aging with so interesting and demanding a God?"

Typical of Scripture, the story of Eli is simply reported without moralization, explanation, or regret. The most thought-provoking character of the narrative isn't grieving old Eli or even up-and-coming young Samuel. The most interesting actor is the author—the God who is in conversation with both Eli and Samuel. Toward the end of our lives, sometimes there is judgment and sometimes blessing, some things work out well for us and others go badly. Our children please and displease. And through it all, a true and living God is free to come and go among us, sovereign, able to reveal or not, calling whom God calls, assigning parts to play in the pageant of God's salvation.

We know how very important friends, social contacts, and interaction with others are for the last quarter of our lives. Yet it is the conviction of the church that of even greater import is our relationship with our most challenging Friend, the One who created us and continues to work with us and to summon us to service even in our old age.

Simeon and Anna, who step on stage and play their parts in welcoming the baby Jesus, Elizabeth and Zechariah, and Abraham and Sarah are not as interesting as the God who speaks and works through them. The central character of the drama is the God of Israel and the church who delights in calling older adults.

In the rest of this chapter, we will explore some of the benefits and the challenges of theological existence, the joy and the pain of lives lived into their last years with faith in the God of Eli, Abraham, Sarah, Zechariah, and Elizabeth.

The Agency of the Aging

Philosopher Martha Nussbaum, in her reflections on the challenges of aging, says that "one of the most damaging of all stereotypes about aging people is that they have no agency; they are just victims of fate." Nussbaum warns, "To rob aging people of agency and choice in the way one describes them is to dehumanize and objectify in a particularly insulting manner."[7]

As a Christian, I'm a bit troubled by Nussbaum's exaltation of human agency as the hallmark of humanity. We Christians believe that we have value because we are created, loved, called, and cherished by God. Our self-worth is due to God's loving agency, not ours. Still, morality implies agency. We generally don't hold people responsible for actions over which they had no control. Ethics is involved in those circumstances in which we ask, "What ought I to do?" Thus the ability to effect change, to impact our situation, to respond, and to exercise agency is a mark of our humanity. Is the inability to act and to effect change in ourselves and our world an inevitable loss of aging?

Harvard's Erik Erikson, in *Identity and the Life Cycle*, says that a major crisis for many elderly is the gap between what they hoped to do in life and what they actually accomplished. If people can creatively deal with that gap, says Erikson, they can reach a high degree of integrity where they can be at peace in a time of life when they are no longer able to accomplish much. If the aged are unable to resolve that conflict, they slip into despair. Later observers corrected Erikson's stark binary by stressing that recognition of a gap between what people hoped to do in life and what they actually did can spur them to strive to give meaning and purpose to the last years of their lives that may have been lacking in earlier years.[8]

Erikson assumes that our aspirations arise solely from within ourselves and our personal ambitions. That's not the Christian view. Through God's vocation, commandeering, and enlistment, ordinary saints are given agency as human extensions of God's divine agency—assigned roles to play in God's work in the world, given something to do for God. Whatever God wants to do in the world, God in Christ has chosen not to work alone.

Through baptism, Christians are not only washed and redeemed but also called, summoned to play our bit parts as coworkers with God. In baptism, we are given lifelong agency as disciples. In a time of life when the purposefulness and meaning that were derived from a job or from caring for a home and family are taken away, the church's conviction that disciples are expected to love and serve God no matter their age can be one of the great gifts of our faith.

One of the challenges of caregiving is to care for the elderly without robbing them of agency. In her discussion of the pros and cons of assisted living arrangements for seniors, Nussbaum says, "We know that an aging individual, as well as the health care system, is better off if assisted living does not infantilize the person, but allows controlling decision-making to remain in the hands of the individual as much as possible."[9]

As part of my training to be a pastor, I took a quarter of clinical pastoral education at Wesley Woods in Atlanta, a care and recuperation facility of the church. At that time, Wesley Woods followed what was called "reality therapy" in which patients were given maximum opportunity to care for themselves and stay in touch with reality. When I, as a student chaplain, entered a patient room, a prescribed dialogue would occur: "Good morning, Mrs. Sheppard. I'm Chaplain Willimon. Do you know what day it is? What time is it?" I would then persist, "Where are you? Tell me the names of your children," and so forth.

We were even encouraged to ask patients questions like, "What is the name of the president of the United States?" The goal was to keep aging minds in reality rather than to aid and abet them in sinking into confusion.

I'm unsure of the effectiveness of this reality therapy in fending off dementia. One man said to me, "Dammit, if you have trouble remembering the name of the president, write it down! I'm not responsible for your forgetfulness!"

I witnessed older persons brought into Wesley Woods on a stretcher, incontinent, unable to feed themselves, totally dependent on caregivers.

Their loving families said things like, "Mama was spilling food on herself when she ate, so we began feeding her." The philosophy of the staff was not to infantilize the patients by spoon-feeding them but to encourage them to feed themselves, even if it took all afternoon.

Within a matter of weeks, many patients were functioning much better. Their families had loved them into passivity and helplessness, robbing them of agency. We must allow and encourage the aged to do as much for themselves as they can and not rob them of the simple joys of self-care, no matter how limited. Above all, as we care for the elderly, we must keep reminding ourselves of the centrality of Christian vocation: Jesus Christ calls ordinary people to discipleship and thereby gives them agency—without regard to their age or stage in life.

Responsible Aging

With agency comes responsibility. The elderly ought to be granted as much agency as possible and then held responsible. The church need not give people a pass on their immorality, abusive behavior, or sins of racism or greed just because they are old. The Fourth Commandment's decree to honor our elders does not mean to honor their mistakes of judgment, abuse of others, or sins.

To tell the truth, Christians are apt to be shaped more by the mores and influences of North American culture than by Scripture. We grow old the American way rather than as Christians. In the literature on gerontology, there is little criticism of the attitudes, prejudices, and biases of older people. Older folks are given a free pass, morally speaking. Yet to rob people of moral evaluation and responsibility is to rob them of their God-given agency. Moreover, it implies that the elderly have no accountability to God. We Christians must be self-critical throughout our lives. My church begins worship on most Sundays with a corporate confession of sin with no age limit on personal and corporate acceptance of blame and responsibility. Some older people have racist views, and those views should not be patronizingly overlooked simply because they have been held for decades. Cruel or abusive behavior must not be excused with "He's just being a dirty old man." The dismissive "silly old fool" is not found in Scripture.

"What gives you the right to cut the taxes that will fund my generation's Social Security?" a twentysomething asked my seventy-year-old senator just after the senator's absurd comment that "climate change is fake news."

Even in our advanced years, we are still called to discipleship, and service in the name of Jesus often entails radical, unceasing personal reformation and sanctification. Older people must be held accountable for their words and deeds, and they must listen to truth-telling younger friends whose honesty God uses to encourage us to greater faithfulness. Sitting passively in the pew—refusing to tell the gospel story, to evangelize, to submit to correction and rebuke by brothers and sisters in the church, and to be engaged in Christ's mission—cannot be an option for aging Christians. Irresponsibility is ugly in a Christian of sixteen or sixty.

Not all elderly are passive, powerless recipients of care; many of the elderly continue to enjoy mobility, material resources, and mental capacities that enable them to be active givers of care and generous responders to the needs of others with their time and money. Pastors should not consign an older member of the church to the list of "homebound" if in most activities (other than church attendance!) that person is active. Being on a fixed income is not reason enough for a person to be excused from financial support of the church's ministries. As a preacher, I need to preach with the conviction that while there's life, it's never too late for a Christian to cultivate generosity, courage, selflessness, and love.

Back in the sixties, it was fashionable for sociologists to interpret aging through the disengagement theory. This theory speculates that as people grow older, both they and the society in which they live agree on their gradual withdrawal from earlier social ties, roles, and responsibilities. The elderly deal with aging by disengagement and detachment from active life as their world shrinks to themselves and their own needs. I vividly remember the pastoral care textbook that told us seminarians that the chief factor in older adult experience is contraction: the aging person disappears from the community to safe confinement in the home, then to life limited to one room in a nursing facility, then to a bed, finally to a coffin, where the family disengages from the older person who disengaged from them.

Disengagement theory has been criticized as a demeaning view of older people, not only at odds with the data on how older adults actually age but also failing to match a more Christian view of humanity. Martin Luther defined sin as "the heart turned in upon itself."[10] Christ teaches his disciples to engage, to love their neighbors, to feed the hungry, to go into the world, to teach, to heal, and to witness without setting age limitations.

Earlier we noted researchers' amazement that when asked how they're doing, most of the aging reply that they are doing well "for my age." Many report that their health is good, even though they face serious health challenges. Does sanguinity about health demonstrate that these elderly are being unrealistic, or does it show that they know enough of God's will for their lives to believe that they are obligated, even amid the health challenges of aging, to positively preserve some sense of agency and responsibility?

There's some truth to the old saw "You are only as old as you feel." Attitude counts. Philosopher Christian Miller cites studies that indicate that an attitude of gratitude has documentable health advantages. People who believe that their lives are gifts—looking back, things have worked out well—tend to enjoy better physical and mental well-being. Miller believes that by cultivating feelings of gratitude, we can live longer and better.[11] Paul's exhortation to "give thanks in every situation" (1 Thess. 5:18) appears to be not only good theology but also good medicine. At our fiftieth college reunion, I asked a classmate how he overcame his alcoholism as late as age sixty. He replied, "I just decided to be happy."

After a visit to a woman in a nursing home (whose adult son was alienated because of her constant complaining and sourness), I said to the son, "I think your mother is depressed. She ought to be examined by a doctor." A mood-altering drug was prescribed. The son later said, "My mother's last years of life were a sheer joy to her and to her family."

However, we should be wary of efforts to drug or to moralize in order to encourage sour, complaining, and angry older adults to look on life more positively. Many older adults have good reason to feel sad. Sometimes older adults, like people of any age, do not handle life's disappointments and regrets in a positive way. It's threatening

for younger people to hear their elders express regrets, disappointments, or anger toward the very projects in which younger people are
investing themselves. Aging can be challenge enough without always
having to be pleasant and upbeat about the realities of growing old.[12]

In *Keep Moving*, Dick Van Dyke, the popular entertainer (writing
in his mid-nineties), says that the most important advice for seniors
is simple: keep moving.[13] The brain craves familiar, effortless ruts and
sends powerful messages to stay put and continue to plow familiar
furrows. For Van Dyke, keeping moving is a moral imperative for the
aged. If we can move, we must. We have a responsibility to ourselves
and to our friends (and to God) to keep moving as long as God grants
us the ability. Being able to boast, "Here all my needs are met; I don't
have to lift a finger" may not be best for the well-being of a resident
of a retirement facility.

The average human life span in the United States is now about
eighty years. Yet the maximum human life span is 120 years. Humans
have one of the largest gaps between average life span and maximum life span when compared with other animals. Lifestyle habits,
the intent to keep moving, diet, time spent interacting and intercon-
nected with others, fulfilling responsibility for someone other than
ourselves—in short, all the choices we make throughout the course
of our lives—sometimes don't impact us until our last decades, when
our chickens come home to roost. The bad habits that we successfully managed in earlier decades get the best of us in our last years,
reducing our longevity.

Most of us don't think of our medical problems as connected to
morality, having long since disposed of the notion that good or bad
things happen to us because of our good or bad actions and attitudes.
Still, an administrator of the Medical School once swept his hand
across the horizon of the vast Duke Medical Center and said to me,
"Well over half of the patients in those hospital rooms are there due
to their lifestyle choices." Agency entails responsibility, and unwise
lifestyle choices are apt to bear their bitter fruit after age sixty-five.

"It's irresponsible for you to refuse to use the handrail on the
stairs," one of my friends said to me.

Even with health problems, the majority of the aged are still able
to manage their own households. Over a third of those living beyond

eighty-five years can be described as fit for independent living, some
with only minimal and occasional assistance.[14] There is no hard-
and-fast rule for the relationship between aging and physical health.
Indeed, there is much variability and variety, possibly due to the differing ways these adults have responsibly exercised their agency or,
to put it in a more Christian way, due to the differing ways these
adults have stepped up to the gifts that God has given them and to
the tasks that Christ has assigned to them.

As we have noted, aging can be experienced as an acceptance of
a life that's increasingly out of our control. Loss of control can be
particularly painful for controlling personalities. The challenge is to
be honest about those factors over which we have control, to let go of
those areas over which we have no control, and to have the wisdom
to know the difference. If wisdom is required for truthfulness about
the God-given agency and responsibility of the aged, as well as our
limits, that's good; the philosopher G. W. F. Hegel said, "The owl of
Minerva [Roman goddess of wisdom] flies at dusk."[15]

Generation to Generation

For Christians, aging is a test of character, a time for witness and therefore an invitation for each of us to be a teacher, to hand over what we
have learned to another generation. We have less time to live, yet most
of us find, in our last decades, that we have more time to give. Not only
do children who are tutored by the elderly in after-school programs
show remarkable progress (because of older adults' patience, focus,
and gift of time?), but the older adult tutors also show measurable
positive changes in their physical and emotional well-being. In giving,
we receive, as someone has said (Luke 6:38).

Among the lessons elders can teach the young are these: the joy of
forgiveness, the gratification to be received through Christian service
to others, the worth of people even when they have dementia, the limits of wealth, and the delight in the old, old story of God with us. On
top of that, older people can show the rest of the church how to die.

Younger people gain from being in community with older adults,
yet sometimes responsibility flows from the young to the old. I was
in a little congregation where the pastor called forward those who

were seeking baptism. An old man hobbled to the front. The pastor embraced him and said with excitement in her voice, "Our young adults group met George in their ministry with those who live on the streets of our town. Until last month, George was living under the railroad trestle off Elm Street. Due to his liver disease, George has only a couple weeks to live. And guess where George has chosen to spend his last days? Here with us!"

The congregation broke into applause.

"George, why don't you tell the church why you want to be baptized?"

George thanked the congregation for their care of him and told them that they made him want to die with Jesus. He had gotten to know the church because of three or four young adults who helped him get medical care. What a credit to this congregation that someone wanted to spend his last days with them. "One generation shall laud your works to another, and shall declare your mighty acts" (Ps. 145:4 NRSV).

Remembering

One of the most prophetic, faith-engendering acts of the church is remembrance. It is sad that older adults are full of memory and yet are subject to memory loss, particularly short-term memory loss. The aging find that the present becomes harder to recall, while the past becomes more easily recollected. Of people over sixty-four, 10 percent suffer from dementia; dementia rates rise to 32 percent in people over eighty-four.[16] I vividly remember my first parishioner to be diagnosed with Alzheimer's disease. Since my pastoral role mostly involved talking, listening, and thinking, I was terrified to see a beloved personality slip away due to loss of memory, and I was in anguish because of my inability to help.

James Woodward gives some guidelines for visiting people with dementia: don't rush your visit, introduce yourself and give some information about yourself every time you meet, sit on the same level as the person you are conversing with, speak slowly and simply but don't patronize or infantilize, allow time for the person to reply, don't be afraid of sustained pauses, ask only one question at a time, visit earlier in the day when the person is less fatigued, and use touch when appropriate.[17]

For the aged, it is usually pleasant to remember, to recollect, to reminisce, and to continue to engage some of the questions and projects that they worked on in the past. The stories of Elizabeth and Zechariah, Simeon and Anna push us to remember that we have more future with a living God than past; God keeps us leaning toward the future, expectant and hopeful that though our lifetimes are ending, God is forever beginning, creating, and venturing. Throughout our lives, it's a challenge not to tuck God comfortably within the past, to make of God a distantly remembered relic rather than a presently resurrected Lord. As Jesus said, God is God of the living and not the dead (Mark 12:27).

History need not enslave. We are free lovingly to recall the past but not to idolize the past. The good old days weren't good for many; that we fail to remember some of the pain of the past may be testimony to the graciousness of forgetfulness. Sometimes the way we recall the past demonstrates our self-deceit.

Every Sunday when the Bible is brought into worship and we read from it and thereby submit ourselves to the wisdom of the ancients, we show the centrality of memory in the Christian life. Scripture holds in memory some of our greatest truths about God and our best adventures with God so that we don't have to. Much of the church's life is in response to Jesus's "Do this in remembrance of me." Yet with a living God who is eschatologically active in the redemption of the world, tomorrow could easily be better than yesterday. One benefit of the Christian practice of forgiveness is that it enables us to begin again rather than to be constantly bound to the past.

Elders' capacity to spend so much of their conversations dredging up the past can be annoying. Maybe aging Christians ought to give ourselves a "remembering budget," budgeting the time that we spend on projects from the past and giving ourselves more fully to undertakings that enrich the present and the future, not only because present and future time for us is dwindling but also because God is with us most vibrantly in the present and the future. In our recollection, self-discipline is required. If, when others are kind enough to pay us a visit, we dominate the entire conversation, repetitiously talking about the past or itemizing our aches and pains, the visit will not likely be repeated.

Suffering

Many of the elderly suffer chronic pain. One of the odd claims of the cruciform Christian faith is that suffering can be redemptive. Somehow the pain of Christ is related to the mystery of the atoning work of Christ, and somehow our pain is part of Christ's atoning work. Paul complained about his painful "thorn in the flesh" but kept on preaching anyhow (2 Cor. 12:7). Christ never implied that following him meant freedom from suffering. In fact, he commanded each of us to take up our cross daily and follow him (Matt. 16:24–26). In aging, some of us will receive what we asked for when we sang the old hymn, "Draw me nearer, nearer, nearer blessed Lord to the cross where thou hast died."[18]

The suffering occasioned by cross-bearing is the pain produced by discipleship, whereas the suffering of the elderly tends to be bodily pain due to the natural processes of aging. Still, the Christian faith neither denies nor promises relief from all pain. Paul dares us to "take pride in our problems, because we know that trouble produces endurance, endurance produces character, and character produces hope. This hope doesn't put us to shame, because the love of God has been poured out in our hearts through the Holy Spirit, who has been given to us" (Rom. 5:3–5). Paul's boasting is not based on a general conviction that all suffering is worthwhile or that pain is positive in its effects but rather because of "the Holy Spirit who has been given to us," we can expect even suffering to be used by a redemptive God.

A little later in his Letter to the Romans, Paul urges endurance in suffering that is based on hope in God's promised future.

> I believe that the present suffering is nothing compared to the coming glory that is going to be revealed to us. The whole creation waits breathless with anticipation for the revelation of God's sons and daughters. Creation was subjected to frustration, not by its own choice—it was the choice of the one who subjected it—but in the hope that the creation itself will be set free from slavery to decay and

brought into the glorious freedom of God's children. We know that
the whole creation is groaning together and suffering labor pains up
until now. And it's not only the creation. We ourselves who have the
Spirit as the first crop of the harvest also groan inside as we wait to
be adopted and for our bodies to be set free. We were saved in hope.
If we see what we hope for, that isn't hope. Who hopes for what they
already see? But if we hope for what we don't see, we wait for it with
patience. (8:18–25)

While this passage speaks of an eschatological hope of future relief
from suffering due to the "coming glory that is going to be revealed
to us," it also candidly acknowledges "the present suffering" (v. 18).
Aging bodies sometimes experience "slavery to decay" that causes
occasional "groaning" (vv. 21–22). Sometimes our suffering becomes
anguish as we regret events from the past or our lack of accomplish-
ment. While there is little of Buddha's dictum that "life is suffering"
in the life-affirming good news of Christ, there is acknowledgment
by Jesus that suffering is the price we pay for embodied life and that
some suffering arises from the world's hostility to Christ and his
followers (Matt. 5:11).

Unfortunately, in our therapeutic culture we have moved beyond
noble attempts to relieve the pain of physical suffering or the agony
of mental anguish and bought into the myth that all suffering is unnecessary, meaningless, and avoidable.[19]

In a small congregation during prayer requests, a person asked,
"Pray for Mama. She has been in pain. I just don't know what this
good woman has done to deserve this."

"His mama is the oldest member of our congregation," the host
pastor whispered to me, "ninety-six years old."

While we ought to pray for the alleviation of someone's suffering,
are there theological dangers in considering pain to be an undeserved
intrusion in a long-lived life? Is the toward-the-end-of-life suffering of a
ninety-six-year-old an injustice? What did Mama do to "deserve" a life
that is twenty years longer than the lives of her fellow church members?
Probably as little as she did to "deserve" this suffering at the end.

There is a prejudice abroad that all suffering is without meaning
and that the prospect of death is inherently bleak and unimaginable.

Christians therefore must find a way to live well without denying suffering and death as aspects of life. Only God is eternal. At every stage of life we are dependent, not on our efforts but on the grace of God. The suffering of Jesus helps to redeem our suffering by knowing "Christ and the power of his resurrection and the sharing of his sufferings by becoming like him in his death" (Phil. 3:10 NRSV). Jesus has not only been through suffering and anguish worse than ours, he is known by his active compassion for sufferers. Where there is suffering, there is Christ.

One caveat: while a theology of redemptive suffering may help with our own anguish, aches, and pains, we should be loath to apply it to the suffering of others. It's not for me (even if Paul did it) to tell some sufferer, "Rejoice, your suffering is a gift from God to draw you closer to God." Still, one can humbly offer a suffering friend the hopeful assurance that, even in suffering, God is there.

Much research is being expended on end-of-life health issues. Is this effort truly health care, or is it immortality fantasy? I fear that some of the impetus for this research comes from our negative attitudes toward suffering and death. Though the goal of palliative care is positively stated as "improving the quality of life," one has the suspicion that the point of much of this care is drug-induced banishment of human pain.

"Because of America's opioid epidemic," said my doctor recently, "our hospital now says upfront, 'Recovery from your surgery is bound to involve some pain. We promise to manage your pain as part of the natural healing process, but recovery without pain is impossible.'"

How can Paul proclaim that he's "happy to be suffering for you"? Paul can boast of happy pain because he is "completing what is missing from Christ's sufferings with [his] own body. [He's] doing this for the sake of [Christ's] body, which is the church" (Col. 1:24).

Though there is no equal correlation between the suffering of Christ and the suffering of Christians, and though the cross of Christ neither explains or explains away all suffering, Jesus's way of suffering service offers us Christians the opportunity to make sense of our suffering and even to see our pain as an expression of our discipleship and thereby to make a witness to the world, which thinks that all suffering is without meaning. Though suffering is rarely a gift of

God to the sufferer or anybody else, the way that we suffer can be a gift to others, our testimonial that life can be lived even in life's pain.

We should certainly avoid suffering, but suffering must not be avoided at all costs. We worship a God who lovingly suffered for us as "a man who suffered, who knew sickness well" (Isa. 53:3). Aging provides the church a grand opportunity to rethink and to reform the life of the church and the lives of individual Christians who are part of the Body of Christ. By the time we are old, while it is not too late to take measures in order to age well, aging is easier if the church has been preparing us all our lives for pain, for aging, and for inevitable death.

Rather than isolate sufferers and hide from view those who are dying, the church compels us to be connected with the suffering of others. Just as Christ was "a man of suffering," Christ embodies suffering love so, where there's suffering, there's Christ, and where Christ is, we want to be.

In all stages of life, Christ must be granted room to work, to work even in our suffering, even in our worst of times, and especially there. There's no way to avoid human suffering, our own or others'. We are animals. More significantly, Christians are walking the way of the cross with Christ. When we suffer, we can take heart in the knowledge that Christ has been there and in knowing that when we find ourselves in pain, we find ourselves with him.

As a pastor, I feel privileged to have seen many dear people suffer and die. I say "privileged" because when it comes my turn to go through pain and death, I hope I'll be able to show what I've learned, asking not, "What have I done to deserve this?" but rather saying, "Now it's my turn to give back the life that God has graciously entrusted to me."

Dependence

Christianity is training in dependency, learning to acknowledge that our lives are tied to the gifts of others and that our salvation is utterly dependent on God doing for us what we cannot do for ourselves. One of the most radical, prophetic acts of my church occurs when we come forward for the Eucharist and are compelled to open our hands to receive the body and the blood. That openhanded physical gesture of emptiness, need, and dependency is countercultural.

Mary Pipher says in the opening of her book *Another Country: Navigating the Emotional Terrain of Our Elders*, "Aging in America is harder than it needs to be."[20] Aging is difficult in a culture that is obsessed with autonomy and self-construction. (No wonder we are a society of widespread loneliness.) The dependence that usually comes with aging and terminal illness can be a Christian witness to the mutual dependence that God intends for us throughout the Christian life. The fond fantasy of the elderly is to remain independent. Yet networks of interdependence (like the local congregation) sustain human usefulness and purpose.

I've stressed that we elderly need not passively waste away in health care facilities; we can be active agents. How much of my stress on agency and initiative betrays how I have bought into less-than-Christian notions of autonomy and independence? Do appeals for the aged to take charge of their aging and get their heads straight about the second half of life contribute to the problem of aging rather than solve it? What do we do in cases when, due to physical deterioration or dementia, there is a dramatic lack of agency? In a culture that worships individual autonomy, the dependence and need of the elderly reveal the lie of human self-sufficiency. Christians are called prophetically to proclaim that Jesus Christ has made everybody interdependent.

> Then the king will say to those on his right, "Come, you who will receive good things from my Father. Inherit the kingdom that was prepared for you before the world began. I was hungry and you gave me food to eat. I was thirsty and you gave me a drink. I was a stranger and you welcomed me. I was naked and you gave me clothes to wear. I was sick and you took care of me. I was in prison and you visited me." (Matt 25:34–36)

Not only do the elderly lose their independence but so do the caregivers to the ill and aging. If autonomy is the mark of a good life, then those who tie their lives to others by providing loving presence and care for the ill and the elderly are diminished. Christians can help their fellow Americans recover the relational character of the good life as opposed to the ideal of the solitary hero or the self-sufficient loner. We are not simply "interdependent"; in a specifically Christian point of view, Christ makes us "mutually dependent." Not only are we subject to God for what we need in order to live, but God has also created us to be dependent, connected to one another, empty-handed as we stand before our sisters and brothers in the Body of Christ. "The parts of the body that people think are the weakest are the most necessary," preaches Paul (1 Cor. 12:22).

Sometimes in our losses God moves us to gratitude for the gifts of friends and allies. Is it possible that our losses are also God's way of ripping some of our idols out of our hands so that we may more fully worship and give ourselves to God? Maybe loss, while a painful part of life and love, can be an occasion for a redemptive God to work with us to enable us to be more grateful for and more truthful about our interconnectedness and interdependence. "Naked I came from my mother's womb; naked I will return there" (Job 1:21).

Loneliness

Loneliness is a state of longing, a feeling of emptiness that is a major aspect of life among the aging, particularly those who age in a culture that bows before the idol of individuality and autonomy.

Loneliness is evidence that God has implanted within us a desire for interaction with others, a longing for loving connection.[21] Sometimes loneliness is proportional to the amount of loss a person has suffered. In other people, loneliness accompanies self-alienation, disappointment, and self-rejection. To be elderly and alone does not automatically mean that one is lonely. Sometimes loneliness can be experienced as grace-filled solitude, a gift, a privilege. The move from loneliness to softer, kinder solitude can be a learned skill of the aged. Thus Richard Rohr says that one of the tasks of successful aging is to learn to be "happy alone" and that the cure for loneliness is to cultivate "the disciplines of solitude."[22]

I know a man who had a very public life as a prominent pastor. I doubt that in his retirement he feels lonely. He has learned to relish solitude and to enjoy being out of the public eye.

A myth of aging is that older adults have no sexuality.[23] While sex and romantic love among the aging are a reality, love among the aging can be complicated. Older people carry baggage into their relationships. Aging people have a past and also a present that often includes ex-spouses and children. The opinions of the children about the marital relationships undertaken by their parents or grandparents can make those relationships difficult. Sometimes stepchildren find it tough to include their aging parent's new partner in a new and blended family.

The Netflix series *The Kominsky Method* is a funny, insightful (some critics say "sad") look at two men who deal with the challenges of aging. After three failed marriages, Sandy Kominsky (Michael Douglas) has nothing to occupy his time except rather ridiculous attempts at affairs with younger women. His friend and agent, Norman Newlander, in deep grief over the death of his wife, is at least steadied in his last years by his Jewish faith. As Newlander repeatedly tells him, Kominsky's bungled affairs show that sex, as good as it can be, is not up to the task of saving us from despair at the work necessary for aging well.

Still, romantic love and sexual activity during the last years of life may be a testimonial that God has created us for community, communion, and partnership and has given us desires that do not end at sixty-five.

In the churches I've served, I've been surprised by a number of divorces of couples over sixty-five, sometimes accompanied by the statement, "I'm retiring. Why not get out of the marriage that has made me unhappy for so long?" Others said, "I liked being married to him when he was on the road most of the week, but can't handle having him home all the time looking over my shoulder."

On the other hand, I have also known three couples who had been divorced for some time but who got back together and cared for each other in their last years, choosing to spend those years together rather than apart.

That so many aging persons choose not to remarry after the death of a spouse may be a testimonial that when marriage has ended by death, the surviving spouse may not feel that he or she is consigned to inevitable loneliness but rather can now have a different sort of life. As a widow said to me, "I loved being married to Tom, but now that Tom is gone, I have no desire to be married to anyone else. Been there, done that."

Others, having enjoyed being married to someone, actively work to stay connected socially and, sometimes, romantically. "I've learned one thing about myself in thirty years of marriage," said one widow. "I enjoy men. I don't like living alone. Pastor, bolster yourself for a round of premarital counseling."

Grief

Grief tends to be an intensely personal experience. As a pastor, I've advised grieving persons, "Grieve as you grieve, not as someone tells you that you ought to grieve."

Although grief among the elderly involves some of the same tasks and is assuaged by some of the same comforts as loss during any time of life, many older people seem to have resources for doing grief work because they have had more experience with loss over their years of life.

First Timothy 5:3 asserts that taking care of widows, women whose husbands have died (or may have been martyred), is a key activity of the church. While marriage is the norm for most aging men, nearly half of women beyond their sixty-fifth birthday are widows. Statistically, older widows tend not to remarry, which may indicate that not all widows are inevitably lonely and unhappy or that initiating romantic relationships and matrimony in our last years isn't easy.[24] Again, it's not helpful to make generalizations about how people grieve or should grieve.

Widowhood requires a person to ask, "Who am I if I am no longer a spouse?"[25] Sometimes the task of widowhood is establishing a new lifestyle or restructuring friendships. The loss of a spouse and the attendant grief must not be seen as a pathology. The grief testifies to love and is a necessary path one must walk after loss toward recovery and readjustment.

As a young pastor attempting to minister to an older woman whose husband had suddenly died, I witnessed other widows giving comfort.

"Sure, this is a blow to you, an adjustment," one said. "But you will come to see the bright side of all this." What?

Said another, "We go to Atlanta shopping three times a year and take a cruise every spring. It's sad that George has died, but welcome to our club!"

(While their comfort may have been reassuring, as their pastor I immediately set out to give this post-marriage club an agenda more important than shopping.)

Gender Differences in Aging

Women live longer than men. The mortality gender gap appears to have social as well as biological reasons. Men in our culture are more prone to have accidents and diseases that could have their roots in men's competitiveness, high-risk activities, and drug and alcohol abuse. Women appear to show greater flexibility and resilience in aging than men. Perhaps that will change with more economic opportunities for women—accompanied by more stress and strain—and with men learning to function in a wider array of roles.

Nearly three-fourths of the elderly poor are women. This disproportionality may be due to the way Social Security is structured, to the pay gap between women and men, or to how women are often penalized through divorce. An economically unjust divorce settlement sometimes does not bear its bitter fruit until old age. Most of the negative burdens of the aged poor, widowed, and those living alone are more characteristic of women than of men.[26]

Aging men often have a deep ambivalence about the aging process, feeling that they have lost purposeful activity and personal significance. Because men often receive less social support in their work in secular settings, the support they receive in the church may be even more important as they negotiate the challenges of aging. Women have less access than men to secular sources of power, prestige, and resources; therefore, they may more highly value the access to power, influence, and leadership that's given them in the church (or feel a special resentment when their church does not grant them this access).

Perhaps that is why, compared to older men, older women are more likely to attend church, pray, and report that religion is important to them. Some research indicates that in the last years of life there is a shift away from the stereotyped roles for men and women to an emphasis on finding wholeness and integration in life. Some researchers even say that in older age gender is psychologically transcended.[27] In aging, some of the limitations imposed on people by social constructs of gender roles can be overcome as men enjoy caregiving and nurturing and women assume more authority in the governance of finances in the household and leadership in church and civic organizations.

Church Participation

There are over 350,000 Catholic and Protestant Christian congregations in America. About 70 percent of Americans consider themselves members of some religious denomination. Nearly 40 percent of the aged claim to attend weekly worship. Ninety percent of adults age sixty-five and under report a religious affiliation. Eighty-four percent of fifty- to sixty-four-year-olds are religiously affiliated. Among African American and Latinx adults in these age groups, the number is about 5 percent higher.[28]

A Barna study in 2002 revealed that approximately 89 percent of older people pray, and about half say they read the Bible during the same week. Fifty-five percent have attended religious services in the past seven days.[29] While older adults may struggle with diminished levels of activity in many areas of their lives, they are the most active religious age group in America.

"Amid an attendance recession," one pastor preached to her congregation, "we're counting on those of you over sixty-five to step up your church attendance. We need you present with us for prayer and praise! Now more than ever! Maybe you can't set up tables for the weekly food giveaway. At least you can show up for worship!"

There is now a *Journal of Religious Gerontology* that regularly reports that older people are deeply immersed in religion. A 1999 study showed that 79 percent of people between the ages of sixty-five and seventy-four claim that religion is "very important." Some research indicates that people do indeed become more religious with age, though there are multiple patterns of religious involvement in the later years, just as in the prior years.[30]

I'm unsure what to make of claims of the beneficent effects of religiosity on elder health. For one thing, it's tough to control for factors outside of a person's religious practices. A fifty-year-old active Mormon who is also a lifelong abstainer from alcohol is probably a candidate for greater longevity. Yet how do we separate his religious beliefs from his abstinence?

Research indicates that religious interest increases with age, but why? George Vaillant notes that the Grant Study found an increase in religious involvement among the subjects of the study, but those who were active in religious practices "manifested nine times as many symptoms of depression, and spent three times as many years disabled, or were dead before age 80." Vaillant theorizes not that religion is bad for mental health but that the depressed and anxious are more likely to seek religious comfort.[31]

Vaillant found scant relationship between physical health and religious involvement. He also found no difference in mortality and no difference in rates of smoking or alcohol abuse among the religiously inclined. Mormons, Seventh-day Adventists, and evangelical Christians live longer than their atheistic neighbors, but they use tobacco and alcohol less. Vaillant's verdict is that "abstinence from drinking and smoking play more of a role in increased longevity than religious devotion itself."[32] Still, "Looked at from a psychosocial perspective rather than a strictly medical one," says Vaillant, "religious devotion remains one of humanity's great sources of comfort, and for many replaces the use (and abuse) 0of alcohol and cigarettes."[33]

Strikingly, Vaillant hypothesized that religious involvement would lead to enhanced social support, but he found little evidence among his Grant Study men that this was true. Still, Vaillant thinks that religious involvement could be a comfort to the lonely—God loves us even when people don't.

"An impressive body of research suggests that attendance at religious services protects against premature mortality," admits Vaillant. However, he found no direct, causal effect. Cigarettes and alcohol are important factors, but they are often only self-reported in studies attempting to link religious observance to physical health. Vaillant wonders if these studies tend to take place in the Bible Belt, where agnostics tend to be "social outliers" anyway. "In samples where healthy social adjustment usually includes clear religious involvement, such involvement is likely to correlate with warm relationships, social supports, and good physical health. Evidence of that correlation, however, does not reflect a direct causal relationship between religious involvement and health."[34]

In 1998, my colleague Harold Koenig founded the Duke University Center for the Study of Spirituality, Theology, and Health. (Pastors and church leaders can find the center's reports on ongoing research, regular newsletters, and insights at https://spiritualityandhealth.duke .edu.) Koenig and his colleague, Douglas Lawson, assert a verifiable connection between religious involvement and better physical health in the elderly: "A steadily growing body of scientific evidence indicates that religious involvement is associated with better physical health, a greater sense of well-being, less depression, and a reduced need for health services, including hospital stays. Hundreds of research studies conducted at our leading institutions seem to indicate that religious beliefs and practices help people of all ages deal better with stress, increase their contact with helpful social-support networks, and discourage activity that has a negative impact on their health: drug and alcohol abuse, smoking, and high risk sexual behavior, which all contribute to disease and disability."[35]

Koenig believes that "religiosity also encourages responsibility, commitment, and concern and generosity toward others." Religious faith and practice enhance the willingness and the ability of elders to provide nonprofessional "healthcare and sustain their emotional support of others on a volunteer basis." Koenig thinks that volunteer elderly caregivers may be the "pivotal factor preventing the complete degradation of our health care system in coming decades."[36] Volunteering is a major contributor to purposeful retirement for many, and as we have noted, there are mutual benefits. Most elderly volunteer through their place of worship, leading Christian gerontologist Neal Krause to declare that "spirituality is the most important motivating factor in senior citizen volunteers."[37]

Research on aging and religion has had the greatest trouble not in defining successful aging but in defining religion. How does one distinguish between religion and spirituality, or religion and a general philosophy of life? Researchers have also had a tough time differentiating between participation in churches and participation in other altruistic civic organizations. How do we know whether or not the older adults who are more involved with religion than those who are young are more active in religious activities simply because they have more time?

Normally, the way research evaluates age differences in religion is by comparing and contrasting levels of religious participation. How do we measure when a person is being "religious"? Research shows that older people are "more religious"—that is, more religiously involved in religious institutions—than younger adults.[38] But not all religious leaders would be comfortable saying that mere frequent church attendance equates with deep faith.

Krause, when researching aging and religion, looked not simply at indicators such as frequency of church attendance and prayer but also at church-based social relationships. Krause found a high degree of church-based social relationships among the elderly. He admits that there are multiple trajectories of religious involvement over the life course and that generalizations about how people age religiously are difficult.[39]

It's tough to separate the effects of religious involvement that can be attributed to God from those that can be attributed to an individual's desire for relationships within the Christian community. Perhaps we need not disconnect these two factors; Christianity is a communal, social, incarnational faith. Krause and Koenig highlight the centrality of social relationships in the church and attribute positive health correlations to these relationships.

Research on race differences among older people shows that older African Americans are more deeply involved in religion than older white people are, and the beneficial effects of religion on health and well-being appear to be more evident among older black people than older white people.[40] Perhaps the Christian faith has provided these black believers with support in the face of the evil of racism, accounting for why the church is still a central factor in African American society in a way that it is not in predominantly white culture. Some observers believe that African American congregations are more supportive of their elderly than non–African American congregations. Many black people are proud that religion helped their ancestors deal with the horrors of slavery and that their churches were at the forefront in dismantling racial segregation in America; therefore, elders are honored.

I am reluctant to make too much of data that say religion is good for our health. Who wants to be utilitarian or an instrumentalist about our faith? Jesus Christ is Lord whether or not worshiping him helps our blood pressure. And while I know that causality can never be determined conclusively with survey data, Koenig's research does seem to confirm what many of us believers have experienced as a gracious by-product of our religious participation: religious and church engagement help us negotiate life's transitions, including the challenges of aging.

Economics

When Hurricane Katrina swept through New Orleans, over one thousand people died, and most of those who died were economically disadvantaged. What's more, 74 percent of those who died were over sixty years old, and 50 percent were over seventy-five, though the elderly constituted only 11.7 percent of the New Orleans population.[41] We have not honored the elderly if we have not confronted the economic systems that oppress them.

For persons of color, aging presents a cumulative economic disadvantage. Limited access to health care, jobs, and education shows up negatively in the bodily experience of older adults. In the United States, one-third of older women live below the poverty line, but for women of color, that number is over 50 percent.[42]

Those of us who have white privilege and who live in an affluent country get to choose all sorts of expensive treatment options and worry about medical dilemmas that are more a function of our affluence than of the improved quality of life produced by our expensive medical care. Sadly, many health dollars go into cosmetic surgical procedures for the affluent aging while many elderly lack access to basic medical care, immunizations, and safe water throughout the life cycle. In our American health care system, those who have accumulated more money get more opportunities to choose how they will age.

Visiting an ailing octogenarian in my congregation as she lay in the hospital, I asked for what she wanted me to pray.

"Pray that my young doctor will leave me alone. That silly boy intends to subject me to therapy that he alleges would give me another two years! If I were twenty, I would take him up on the offer. Why consume resources that could be used on those who are younger? It's not 'health care'; it's death denial. No thanks. I've had enough."

Economic issues not only raise questions about a more just distribution of resources but also prompt us to remember Jesus's judgments about the perils of wealth. Wealth, in the teaching of Jesus, is a problem, not only because it tends to be distributed unequally and produces a sense of entitlement and privilege among the rich but also because it is an encouragement toward idolatry and a corruptor of character. Wealth enables us to make even good health care an idol as we allow our fear of dying, rather than our fear of God, to dominate our imaginations. Visiting the sick and caring for the dying are difficult in a world in which most of us work most of our lives and have little time to expend in care for others. We would rather earn money to pay for care of those we love than do the caring. The burden of the elderly is a problem, not so much because there are so many more elderly in need around us but rather because we are living lives of self-aggrandizement in which there is little time to respond to the needs of others. In short, the crisis in elder care is a call for the church to help us think not only about the aging but also about the inadequate ways we have constructed our lives on mammon rather than on God.

Greed is ugly at sixteen or at sixty. Jesus had some choice words for those who vainly say to themselves, "You have stored up plenty of goods, enough for several years. Take it easy! Eat, drink, and enjoy yourself" (Luke 12:19). We might call someone wise who prudently planned for retirement and stored up treasures for himself; Jesus, in this parable, calls him "fool" (v. 20). The church at its best saves us from foolish lives.

Politics and Social Policy

The challenges of aging are neither purely personal nor exclusively related to getting along well with one another in the church. There are structural, political, social policy reasons for why many find aging difficult. We need those who require care and their caregivers to have more independence, choice, dignity, and control over care. There must be fair access to care and development of preventive services. Health care services should be evaluated on the basis of performance, quality, and waste. Somehow we must come up with resources to care for people with dementia without overwhelming health care systems. And we need to encourage seniors to be active and healthy in their habits and exercise programs.

A society fails to be minimally just if it doesn't secure a basic level of human rights and capabilities for all of its citizens. Drug companies should demonstrate that they are truly reinvesting their profits in research. Health care workers ought to receive just compensation for their labor. Health for the aging is not just about treatment for sickness but also about nutrition, recreation, exercise, and wellness care for injuries. The elderly must be granted access to parks and recreational facilities. Public transportation is extremely important for the well-being of the elderly. The dominance of the car in our culture and the corresponding lack of safe bikeways and walkways are significant challenges for older people and evidence of poor social policy.

Being a Burden

Thinking about aging as a Christian enables the church to confront the widespread American myth that it is possible to live our lives without being a burden, free from being anyone's responsibility. Christians are those who have taken on the burden of Christ's yoke in response to his invitation to come to him, all who are weary and burdened, to receive rest (Matt. 11:28). Strange that Christ promises rest and unburdening by asking us to wear his yoke and take on his burden, for his yoke is easy and his burden is light (vv. 29–30). Christ calls us not to totally unburden ourselves but rather to cast off the baggage that the world puts on our backs in order that he may lay on us his yoke and his burden. Rather than free us from all burdens, Christ gives us burdens worth bearing, lives worth living. Paul characterizes burden-bearing as a "law" of Christ: "Carry each other's burdens and so you will fulfill the law of Christ" (Gal. 6:2). Think of Christianity as training in the assumption of burdens that the world tells us are not our responsibility but that Christ makes our means of serving him.

To take on the yoke of Christ is to be yoked to his Body, the church. We not only are given responsibility for others but also must learn how to be the responsibility of others. Which is more difficult: to give help or to receive help? In our culture, it is grace to be able to say to another, "I need your aid," to allow someone to fulfill Christ's command to "carry each other's burdens." Christianity teaches us how to be a burden to others to whom we have no connection other than baptism.

"Is it fair for you to move your mother into your apartment and assume total responsibility for her?" I asked one of my church members.

"She did that for me when I needed her. Thank God I get to care for the one who cared enough to bring me into this world." Such is the reasoning of those who have taken on the burdens of Christ.

When I praised a woman in my church for showing up at the nursing home every day to care for the needs of an older man from our congregation who had no family nearby, she said to me, "Just this morning I thanked Joe for allowing me to love him in this way. I fail in so many ways to be a faithful Christian. By allowing me to help in his time of need, Joe enables me to be so much better than I would have been on my own."

In Christ, none of us can say, "I'm on my own." We, a burden to a loving God, are called to assume the burdens of others and to let Christ make us a burden to them. The church ought to give us experiences of this burden-bearing as preparation for aging. It is good for us to train our children and grandchildren to be caregivers and to give them opportunities to be with aging persons. To give care and to receive care can be downright prophetic acts in a society that exalts independence over interdependence.

Because of the dread of growing old, there is a widespread rejection of the gift of years. Some opt out. The suicide rate is high among the elderly, particularly elderly men. Suicide rates for the elderly are high in a climate in which we have nothing to do with our dependence, our suffering, and our dying. In baptism, however, our lives are shown to be God's possession and our bodies gifts in service of God and the world. "I have been crucified with Christ and I no longer live, but Christ lives in me" (Gal. 2:20). Appeals to the sacredness of life are not the point. Life is not our possession to be preserved at all costs or expended as we see fit. Nor are debates about "quality of life" much help. Many times, arguments for physician-assisted suicide imply that our suffering has no meaning for ourselves or for others. These ethical debates must be resolved by Christians first asking theological questions like, "Who has God created us to be?" and "What are human beings for?"

A SERMON

Here's a sermon I preached some years ago in an attempt to help my congregation think about these matters.

The Blessedness of Being a Burden[43]

> How can we thank God enough for you, given all the joy we have because of you before our God? (1 Thess. 3:9–13)

In my pastoral care of people who are in the last years of their lives, I have noted that when people face declining health or physical infirmities, it's not death they fear; it's the dying. What they fear is a long dying. More specifically, they fear "becoming a burden on my family." Our prayer is to end our lives in such a way that we will never be a bother to other people by the manner of our leaving.

I've got a couple of children; do I want to be a burden to them in my old age?

Well, why not? They have been a burden to me. True, I did not give them birth, but I was there, close by, and I had to pay for it. Then the diapers, of which I have changed a few. And the sitting in sweltering hot sun at swim meets. And the PTA meetings! How many times I've had to rearrange my schedule to accommodate them. They were a daily burden to us for about twenty years. Even though they've fled the home, I still worry about them. Why should I bother being a burden to them for the couple of years of my dying?

Being a burden is what it means to be in a family. It's part of the price we pay for loving and being loved.

We live in a society that, under the tutelage of the philosophical mistakes of people like John Locke and Thomas Jefferson, tell us that we live under some invisible "social contract" where we autonomous individuals have decided to come together in contractual agreement with one another in order to better gratify our personal desires. Maybe that is enough for a nation; it certainly isn't enough for a family. Being a family means to have claims on one another. Love tends to seek out burdens rather than to avoid them.

Love teaches us that we are never more human than in those moments when we joyfully burden ourselves with other people. To avoid or reject such burdens is to turn our back on our own humanity.

It is the nature of love to expose us to the needs of others, to have our lives interrupted, detoured, and, in general, disrupted by another. We are at our best as we respond to such unchosen, undecided, unplanned demands, interruptions, and encumbrances.

To say that your life is totally free of the bothers and burdens of other people is another way of saying, "I am lonely. I have no better purpose for my life than my life." On one occasion, Jesus told us, "Come to me, all who labor and are heavy laden, and I will give you rest. . . . For my yoke is easy, and my burden is light" (Matt. 11:28, 30 RSV). I find it interesting that Jesus at that moment did not say, "Come to me, all who labor and are heavy laden, and I will relieve you." Rather, he said, "Come to me and I will put a yoke around your necks and place a burden on your backs that you have not previously borne." Sure, his yoke may be "easy" and his burden "light," but a burden is a burden. Jesus seems to have taught that the burdened life is the abundant life.

Think of the church as training in laying down so many of the burdens that our society places on our backs—financial success, the relentless attempt at unbridled personal autonomy, and the constant care of ourselves—in order to bear burdens that we would never have borne before we met Jesus.

I remember that Sunday when, at the close of the service, this woman in my church came up to me and said, "Aren't you bothered that we don't really pray for anybody except ourselves? We pray for those among us who are in the hospital, who are going through difficulties of various kinds. Didn't Jesus tell us to pray for our enemies? Doesn't Jesus expect us to consider as brothers and sisters people we don't even know?"

She was right.

This doesn't mean that attempts to make a living will or advance directives are bad. Nor does it mean that we are wrong to seek help and assistance in caring for those parents or children whose lot in life makes them peculiarly vulnerable and in great need of intense and constant care.

It means that Jesus compels us toward a deep awareness of the interdependence of human life. Not one of us is an island unto ourselves. Our children need adults who are willing to order their lives to care for the needs of children. We older adults need children who are willing, as adult offspring, to order their lives so that they have the blessing of returning some of the love to us that we showed to them when they were dependent. And all of us need to be needed. It's the way God put us together.

Christians are crazy enough, looking at ourselves and others through the eyes of the self-giving love of Jesus, to refer to such "burdens" as God-given blessings.

One of the reasons we flee from the burdensome care of those who are dependent on us is that their sickness, mental or physical infirmity, or incapacity is a reminder of a truth we have so many ways of avoiding—namely, that *all of us are dependent*, that all of us in our lives march toward some final incapacity. Most of us hope that we may die in such a way that we may never know that we are actually dying—quickly, painlessly, with no messy leftovers. The truth is, most of us will die attached, not simply to some medical machine but to other people.

The last days of our lives are even more dependent and burdensome to other people than our first days as infants. I hope that my children, my spouse, and my friends will have pity on me when I am in such circumstances. I expect that they will be far more patient, and wiser, in caring for me in this state than I have been with them. My being a burden to them is the price they pay for love.

And because of their Christian faith, they have been told, if not by me then at least by the Bible, that they are indeed their brothers' and sisters' keepers. Jesus told a story that says those who have loved the most burdensome, "the least of these," have also loved him (Matt. 25).

A man in my church spent most of his life unmarried. He loved to dance. At a ballroom dancing convention, he met a lively woman who shared his love for dancing.

They were always in church on Sunday mornings, but on most Friday or Saturday nights, they danced. I'm talking ballroom, square, South American—you name it, they danced it.

Then one day he called from the hospital to say that her fever was a sign of a terrible illness of the central nervous system. In just a couple of days, she was bedridden, never to walk again. Certainly, never to dance again. Victor changed his work schedule so that he could be home four days a week to care for her. He secured some wonderful care from other persons to help with her. For *six years* he watched over her, loving her, helping her to adjust, organizing parties and dinners at their home where guests gathered around her bedside and laughed and talked, because this brought her joy.

When she died, the church gathered and gave praise to God for her life and witness, and for Victor's as well. During the service, I embarrassed him by making him stand as I said, "Victor, you know how proud we are of you. As your pastor and preacher, I want to take some credit for the way you have lived your life during this difficult time. This church doesn't have many successes. We give thanks to God that you're one of them."

After the funeral and committal, Victor said to me, "Difficult time? That isn't how I would put it. Sure, there were days when I wondered if I could keep going, if I would be able to do for her all that was needed. But you forget. I spent forty years of my life alone. I spent most of my life without anybody who needed me. She made my life count. She gave me a reason for living. She was always much more of a gift than a burden."

I pray to God for such character. I pray for you too. One day may somebody be a great bothersome burden for you. And one day may you be a burden to another as well, thus being the means of someone finding life, and that abundantly.

In the name of Christ, amen.[44]

Bodies

Aging reintroduces us to our bodies. Through much of my life I've treated my body as if it were a car. It gets me from here to there. And when there are malfunctions, I want the problem fixed quickly and effortlessly. Older people are likely to be consumed with bodily health issues because, for older people, suddenly the bodies that we may have neglected—or, conversely, been fastidious in tending—remind us that we are creatures. No matter how good we have been to our bodies, abstemious in our habits, our bodies begin to show signs of age. So there is much conversation about the virtues of our doctors and the search for the surefire cure. As one preacher put it, we engage in "organ recitals" as we detail the liabilities of our aging bodies. When we're in our cohort, we can always talk about our bodies since that's the one thing that unites us.

Yet to despise aging bodies is to despise both our Creator and ourselves as God's creations. We deny our kinship with animals and repudiate our animal weaknesses and vulnerabilities, including our animal-like physical degeneration. The human body decays and smells as it decays. Therefore, to confront aging bodies is to confront tangible, physical truth about ourselves.

Are there limits for the medical treatment we should seek to alter the appearance of our aging bodies? Are facelifts okay? I don't know much about the ethics of cosmetic surgery, but Martha Nussbaum gives some helpful guidelines: we should not use cosmetic procedures as substitutes for exercise and good diet. You must find a way to make peace with the "you" that your body has become. It's sad when Botox, badly applied, prohibits us from smiling. Cosmetic surgery may be a waste of resources when there are better things to do with our money. Surgery is always risky and can have a long and difficult recovery period. Nussbaum says we should be guided by the principle that "looking better is what we're talking about, not looking younger."[45]

The Body of Christ is made up of different kinds of bodies, including older, aging bodies. God's vocation addresses us throughout the life cycle but in diverse ways depending on our stage of life. At twenty, I felt called to be a pastor. At seventy, I still feel called to be a pastor, but I am not called to be the pastor I was at twenty. Paul talked about the church, the Body of Christ, as being made up of diverse vocations, without any one part of the Body being superior in its functions to another. Our work for God is largely dependent on, and often restricted by, what our bodies can do at a given age. Aging requires us realistically to adapt to what our bodies can do for God at a particular time in life. Our response to God's vocation must be repeatedly renegotiated as we prayerfully ask ourselves, "What is God doing with my life and my body now?"

Death

Church is one of the few places in this death-denying culture where we can actually talk about the end. Church is where we name what is important and what is unimportant, where we are given a lens to look at life *sub specie aeternitatis*, a position from which to take the long view. Our lives are bounded, terminal. God has created us as finite creatures who will die. Psalm 90:3–12 speaks of human mortality as an aspect of God's wrath on our iniquity, part of the distance between us and God.

> You return people to dust,
>   saying, "Go back, humans,"
>   because in your perspective a thousand years
>   are like yesterday past,
>   like a short period during the night watch.
> You sweep humans away like a dream,
>   like grass that is renewed in the morning.
> True, in the morning it thrives, renewed,
>   but come evening it withers, all dried up.
> Yes, we are wasting away because of your wrath;
>   we are paralyzed with fear on account of your rage.
> You put our sins right in front of you,
>   set our hidden faults in the light from your face.
> Yes, all our days slip away because of your fury;
>   we finish up our years with a whimper.
> We live at best to be seventy years old,
>   maybe eighty, if we're strong.

But their duration brings hard work and trouble
    because they go by so quickly.
    And then we fly off.
Who can comprehend the power of your anger?
    The honor that is due you corresponds to your wrath.
Teach us to number our days
    so we can have a wise heart.

While death may be a fact of our lives, it is also a sign that the world did not end up as God intended. Though Scripture does not look on aging as an evil or an injustice, that is not the case with death. Jesus certainly agonized over his own death as he prayed in the Garden of Gethsemane to be granted a way out. Jesus grieved at the tomb of his friend Lazarus (John 11:33–37). Judith and Richard Hays say that the New Testament confronts death with the affirmation that "God will overcome the power of death by the resurrection of the body at the last day. The resurrection of Jesus is both the first fruits of his final resurrection and the sign of the eschatological resurrection, in which all Christ's people will share,"[46] remembering Paul's words in 1 Corinthians 15:20–28. And yet we still grieve at the thought of confrontation with "the last enemy" (v. 26).

Christians must find a way to combine honesty about our dying with hope of our resurrection. Resurrection hope lies at the heart of the way Christians embody the practices of growing old. Jesus triumphs over death and, in one great, victoriously loving act, takes us along with him in resurrection. This affirmation frees us from the paralysis that often comes with the fear of death. We need not deceive ourselves about death, nor should we allow the thought of death to overpower our imaginations. The Christian faith gives us the ability to look at death directly but also relatively. Indeed, one might think of Christianity and its funerals, its practices and rituals like baptism and the Lord's Supper, and its reading and preaching of Scripture as training in how to die in the name of Jesus. "Since we believe that Jesus died and rose, so we also believe that God will bring with him those who have died in Jesus. . . . So encourage each other with these words" (1 Thess. 4:14, 18). That statement could be repeated every time the church gathers.

"The truth about life is that we shall die," said writer Philip Roth, just before he died. (Roth spoke of aging as a "massacre."[47]) One reason for stigmatizing the elderly or avoiding attendance at their funerals is that we live in a death-denying culture that is loath to be reminded of life's limits or death's ubiquity. If we reject the assurances of the Christian faith, why not deny or deceive ourselves about death and refuse to face death as a part of life since almighty death has the last word on life?

Death may be "the last enemy to be brought to an end" (1 Cor. 15:26); still, it is an enemy vanquished and being put down by the resurrected Christ, an ultimate defeat to which we can bear prophetic testimony right now by the way we live our lives.

In a death-denying world, older Christians can be teachers, serving as examples of how to age and die well. The young can honor the vocation of the elderly by asking them to tell their stories and by promising to remember and to retell their stories after the elderly have died. As Cicero said, "The burden of age is lighter for those who feel respected and loved by the young."[48]

We must not give death a victory it doesn't deserve. Despair is not permitted among those who know the truth about our end as eternal fellowship with God. The young can remind the old that aging is not an excuse for irresponsibility, indifference, or nihilism. The old can show the young that if we live our lives in fear or denial of death, we deprive ourselves of both living the good life and dying the good death. The Christian faith gives us something worth living for and a divine-human relationship worth dying into.

Without resurrection hope, one is forced to concede that Franz Kafka was right: "The meaning of life is that it stops."[49] Christians know the truth not only that life is terminal, that it stops, but also that even mortal life can have meaning because life with God is not over and done with until God says it is.

The dying of many older people is consumed with regret for things done and left undone. Regret is bound to be present where there's death because too many modern Americans believe that our actions are the only actions, our agency is the only agency. We believe we must strive and produce because solely by our efforts do we ensure that our lives are worth living. We think it's an injustice for creatures so wonderful as ourselves to age and die because it's up to us to make the world turn out right. We've got the whole world in our hands. Amid such delusion, even the most accomplished lives are bound to feel unfinished and regrettable when God is inactive and everything is left up to us.

So as we come to the boundary of our lives, it's good to be reminded that Jesus asserted, toward the end of his earthly life, "My father is still working, and I am working too" (John 5:17). We are creatures who are loved by an active Creator; we are not lonely, frantically driven sole creators. To believe that God is eternal though we are not is to have hope that though our earthly, human work is coming to a close, God's work is continued by God and by God's creativity among coming generations. As Charles Wesley purportedly said, "God buries his workers but carries on his work."

Moses lived to the ripe old age of 120 and still died without entering the promised land (Deut. 31:1–7). Martin Luther King Jr. recalled Moses's death before his life work was completed in his "I've Been to the Mountaintop" sermon the night before he died, confident in his resurrection faith that though his work for racial justice in America was incomplete, God's intentions are not forever defeated. Though King would not get to the "promised land," he had faith that by God's grace, his people would.

Paul admits that death causes grief. We grieve, but because of Christ's continuing victory, we "won't mourn like others who don't have any hope" (1 Thess. 4:13). Nor do we age like those who don't have hope. The God who related to us and summoned us in younger days continues to summon and to employ ordinary people to be the Body of Christ in motion, regardless of age, preparing us for our ultimate vocation—to die in the Lord.

For those of us who have lived out a natural life span, our goal should be palliative care of suffering, not a vain attempt to extend life through Promethean medical interventions. Suffering is the price we pay for the gift of embodied life. Medical resources should not be expended in vain on heroic efforts to achieve an eternal life that only God can give. Death is not an unjust intrusion into life nor a pathology that through extensive, expensive research may be conquered and cured. Death is the way that God set up human life, a boundary that can be overstepped only by God.

When Pope John Paul II refused to go back into the hospital during his final illness, he let himself die. That's not euthanasia; it's withholding heroic treatment, an acceptance of the inevitable, and a refusal to make an unrealistic attempt to postpone the end. As Psalm 90 says, we should "number our days" (v. 12)—know that we are terminal—in order to find a way to wisdom.

When I served as bishop, I discovered the empowerment in knowing the day and the hour when my episcopacy would end, when I would hand over my few achievements and all my frustrations to a successor. Knowing my termination date lent urgency to some of my projects. It also helped to lessen some of the stress caused by my opponents and critics: "There will be a day in August of 2012," I would tell them, "when the Lord will deliver me of you and you will be free of me, though I doubt you will be much happier."

Contemplating the reality of our dying can have a similar effect on our living. We older adults may not know the exact date of our termination, but God gives us opportunities to realize that one day our days will end and that we must entrust our work into the hands of our successors and our lives into the hands of the loving God who gave us life.

Besides, nothing in the Christian tradition leads us to regard biological life, its continuance or its comfortability, as an absolute good that must be sought at all costs. Aging and dying look quite different from the standpoint of the church, the communion of saints.

Memory

On All Saints' Day the church gathers with the dead. We name all those who told us about Jesus and who walked with Jesus in such a way that we wanted to walk with Christ too. The communion of saints comprises the church. Remembrance of and gratitude for the saints keep the church from being reduced to the merely present moment and the church's membership from being limited to those who currently sit in the pews. The church recalls its dead through time, honors their bodies in its funeral practices, and looks forward by looking back. Thus, the church is a community of memory. Memory enables us to see God acting through time, making historians of us all.

In my attempts to lead my church to greater vitality, to reach out to the next generation in order for the denomination to have a future, I learned the importance of having people in the room who could remember when the United Methodist Church was not in decline. Without those who remembered when the church was more faithful in its mission and evangelism, the church was in danger of acquiescing to death and decline as our fate.

When history is considered to be superfluous bunk, the gifts of continuity that the elderly bring to a congregation are undervalued. My first week as the new pastor of a congregation, I always visited the older members first. This won me points. After my visit, these folks would phone their friends and say, "Our nice young pastor visited me today." More importantly, I would say to them, "Tell me how this congregation got to where it is today. What do I need to know about this congregation in order to be an effective pastor here?"

In Plato's *Republic*, Socrates says, "I enjoy talking with very old people. They've gone before us on the road by which we, too, may have to travel, and I think we do well to learn from them what it is like."[50] The stories about the past, told by the elders, point the young into the future. The Christian community can move forward by being critiqued by the memory of the community. To gather on Sunday and to submit to the discipline of remembrance that is entailed in the reading of Scripture is to risk prophetic judgment on the present church. At the same time, we ought to admit that memory can be unreliable, corrupted by nostalgia and sentimentality. Christian community can become closed and introverted, bound to the past that was or never really was.

Sometimes elderly tellers of tales keep a congregation stuck in unhealthy narratives of the congregational past as they tirelessly (and tiresomely) reiterate past injustices or controversies in the congregation.

"This church is still suffering from the damage done here by Pastor Smith," said a church member during her new pastor's first visit to her apartment.

"Pastor Smith?" she asked. "When did he serve here?"

"From 1958 until 1962," she said. "Bad years for us."

"I was in junior high then," the pastor responded glumly.

Though I'm uncertain how wisdom is attained, it's clear to me that the acquisition of years does not correlate directly with the

accruing of wisdom. "No fool like an old fool," we say. Do we have
any evidence to suggest that our election of a president who was over
seventy meant that we were electing a wise person? King Solomon
was wiser as a young person than when he grew old and became as
foolish as King Lear. Vaillant surmises that Jefferson, Gandhi, King,
Mohammed, Lincoln, Tolstoy, and Shakespeare all reached the pin-
nacle of their wisdom between ages thirty and fifty.[51] Still, Methodist that I am, I must add that John Wesley labored in the vineyard
of the Lord right to the end, praising God through his ninety-first
year.

I remember, as a child, that my mother loved watching a TV show
called *Life Begins at Eighty*. Host Jack Barry led a panel of octogenarians who answered questions sent in by viewers at home. *Life Begins
at Eighty* died in 1956 and had no successors. What does that tell you
about the public's thirst for the wisdom of the aged?

Vaillant cites a study called the Mature Reflective Judgment Interview, which found that there is an increase in wisdom up until age
thirty-five. After that, researchers found no strong evidence for further wisdom growth.[52] Yet, who would deny that judges, baseball
managers, cooks, and pastors can grow in wisdom with decades of
seasoning? That pop movies portray and adore the Obi-Wan Kenobis,
Gandalfs, and Dumbledores suggests a widespread longing for wise
elders, a role I'm only too happy to play! Virginia Woolf, in *Mrs. Dal-
loway*, says of one of the elders in her story, "The compensation of
growing old . . . was simply this: that the passions remain as strong
as ever, but one had gained—at last!—The power which adds the
supreme flavor to existence—the power of taking hold of experience,
of turning it around, slowly, in the light."[53]

Not all elderly are wise or have wise stories to tell. And yet congregations are dependent on having a few wise among them to nar-
rate the good and the bad. A new church pastor, when asked what
he most needed to succeed at a church plant, replied, "I never felt I
would be saying this. I've spent much of my ministry complaining
about traditionalist, conservative, older people in my church. But
right now, our trendy twentysomething church could use about a half
dozen traditionalist, history-bearing elders to help us steady ourselves
and move forward." Older people, at least some older people, must

be good at telling stories in order for a community to nourish and refurbish its identity and thereby to survive and thrive.

"Change is unsustainable when it is not rooted in the core identity and basic stories of a congregation," says veteran church observer Lovett Weems Jr.[54] Dean Greg Jones speaks to those of us at Duke on the need for "traditioned innovation," combining two words we don't often hear together. If an innovative pastor wants change to stick, that pastor had better honor the traditions, stories, and enduring values of a congregation (i.e., listen to the stories told by the elders).

When I was bishop, I was surprised to hear some of my older pastors complain, "The bishop is prejudiced against old pastors." I was sixty-five myself. How could I think negatively of older people? As I reflected on their complaint, I had to admit that, in my drive to innovate and improve the church, I had run roughshod over what many of them loved about their churches. When I said, "We ought to change *x*," they heard me devaluing the institution they had given their lives to produce. Perhaps if I had aimed for innovation that was "traditioned," more of the change I wrought would have endured.

Some of us like to think of ourselves as "progressive." Every day we are getting better and better in every way. But this notion of progress, this naively optimistic view of history so prevalent in the West carries with it an incipient rejection of aging. Labeling ourselves progressive implies that we are leaving behind something that is less important, inadequate, and backward and progressing toward something of greater value.[55]

"Progressive Christianity" implies that somehow we are moving onward from insufficient ideas to better ideas, from benighted, superficial faith to more advanced, more satisfactory faith. The Western notion of progress and forward development of history could be a source of some of our debilitating stereotypes of elderhood. Christ is not a historical figure that we can rise above or go beyond; he is the Lord of all, whom we are still trying to comprehend and to catch up with. Christians believe that time does not rise in an upward spiral, an ascending ramp, but rather has a beginning and an ending with God.

The meaning and significance of our lifetime is not solely within our hands. Time is constantly being punctuated and guided by God's activity, *kairos*, when the grace and judgment of God turn our time into God's time. At every stage of life, including the last, our *chronos* can become God's *kairos*. God is determined to have us at each stage of life, especially the last.

Church is inherently traditional and tradition-bearing; we need not thoughtlessly jettison the wisdom of the saints from the past. Yet church is also where we are always being drawn toward a living God; we need not cower before the new and the innovative.

When I go to the doctor's office, I must fill out my health history on an electronic tablet. Nearly all my shopping is online now. When I resumed teaching at Duke Divinity School after being bishop, I was required to take two days of classroom technology training. It's somewhat comforting, in a fast-paced technological age, that church is the one place in my life that is essentially unchanged. Forgive me for being really peeved when my pastor substitutes "Edelweiss" for the traditional tune of the Doxology.

Theologian David Matzko McCarthy reflects on the interplay, and sometimes the tension, between continuity and change in the Christian community.[56] Confronted with physical decline and the loss of loved ones, we aging are tempted to attempt to maintain a sense of sameness and continuity. We spend so much time recalling the past in a vain effort to save the people and the relationships that we loved from the ravages of forgetfulness. Little wonder that many older persons love their church as a place where memory is valued and encouraged and the pews are securely bolted to the floor.

And yet we worship and serve a resurrected, living Lord who is always striding before us into the future. McCarthy notes:

> Generational continuity is essential to the church, which by definition includes the unity of all generations, and all times and places in communion with God . . . in a great company of all who have been drawn into God's self-giving. This community always makes us much more than we would have been otherwise. . . . This coming out and going beyond ourselves, is the pattern of grace. . . . Because the church is bound in time, however, change is inevitable and necessary. Issues of continuity and change are, for Christians, issues about the life of the church and its identity as a people of God.[57]

The Christian church lives by continuity, by remembrance, following God into the future by what we know of God's actions in the past. Traditioning—introducing the young to the old, old gospel story; lovingly reiterating the core of our faith; and taking up the habits required for holy living—is a major activity of the church whereby the church makes its existence intelligible. The primary reason for remembering and traditioning is to equip ourselves to keep up with the machinations of a living God.

As I was becoming a bishop, I sought advice from retired bishops. Most of them remembered the episcopacy as a frustrating, well-nigh futile undertaking in which they were constantly thwarted by constituencies as well as by the restrictions of church law.

Yet a few of the retired bishops I interviewed remembered their time of leadership as demanding but rewarding ministry. I asked one, "Why do so many of the retired bishops tell me that the job is impossible?"

"That's how some older bishops excuse their own ineffectiveness," said the wiser retired bishop.

It's good for the young to seek the advice of the aged. And yet our memories should be received and evaluated with a degree of skepticism, for memory can be selective and self-serving, if not self-deluding.

At the beginning of the semester I tell my seminarians, "I've been in ministry a long time. I'm going to share with you some of the lessons I've learned and some of the mistakes I've made. I hope you will find my memories to be helpful. However, not all of my wisdom will have value. You can't serve the church that I served. You'll have to profit from some of my memories and dispose of the rest so that my memories won't keep you tied to the old order, which you'll need to leave behind as you press on."

One reason the aging remember is to preserve a now-disintegrating sense of self. We remember selectively, even desperately, defiantly, having lost a job and some of our friends and family. Remembrance is an act of defiance against injustice, recalling the lives of past victims in order that their witness not be lost. Is my sleep so full of dreams these days because my mind is frantically attempting to retrieve and relive bits of a past that's now slipping away?

Sometimes we must selectively recall because past hurts are too debilitating to be remembered. While the forgiveness that Jesus commands is more complex than "forgive and forget," there is an element of forgetfulness in true forgiveness. We forget past wrongs done to us because we remember Christ's command to forgive our enemies. Nurturance of grudges and remembrance of past slights saps the life out of us, so it's better willfully to forget than to remember.

And yet some of our feverish attempts to hold on to our memories may be a sign that we fear we are being forgotten. We may have bought into the widespread American notion that the way to have a self is constantly to construct, to reconstruct, and to present the ideal self (these days, presented through social media), seeing ourselves as the sum of our efforts rather than as a gift of God's love and vocation. Our hope is not in our or others' ability to preserve the memory of who we "really are"; rather, our hope is that a resurrecting God remembers us. The psalmist prays, "Remember me!" (Ps. 25:7).

In a sermon on Psalm 25:7, "Remember Not the Sins of My Youth, Remember Me," Elizabeth Achtemeier recalled a self-important faculty colleague who had no time to waste with her when she was a struggling young professor; he was writing important books, and she was only a young woman in a man's world. "As he lay dying, I visited him in hospital. Comatose, tubes coming out of his nose. His wife had stacked his four books on the bedside table to comfort him." Achtemeier paused for effect, tilted toward the congregation, stared them down through her granny glasses, and took her voice down to a threatening whisper. "Friends, when you die, you die, and all that you proudly created dies with you. If God forgets to take you along into eternity, *you are without hope*."

Remembrance of God's remembrance of us is an important insight that can help us when loved ones are diagnosed with or suffer from dementia. In Christian funerals, we remember those who have lost minds and lives and whose bodies have disintegrated. They are remembered by the community and, more importantly, by God. Their existence, though radically changed, ends not if God remembers—that is, resurrects.

God's promised resurrection remembrance of us is our great hope and comfort as Christians, particularly in seasons of life when we are prone to forgetfulness. Sometimes the church remembers on behalf of those who are losing their mental capacities, prays for those who can no longer pray, believes for those who are being tortured by doubt, and witnesses publicly for those who no longer speak.

Membership in the Body of Christ never comes as a personal achievement but as a gift, an invitation from God, an adoption into the community. The elderly—who feel that their opportunities for individual achievement are diminished—can be living, bodily reminders to us all that our lives are not the sum of our attainments, never our sole possessions, but rather, from birth to death, God's gifts.

SIX

Growing Old in Church

As [Jesus] was teaching, he said, "Watch out for the legal experts. They like to walk around in long robes. They want to be greeted with honor in the markets. They long for places of honor in the synagogues and at banquets. They are the ones who cheat widows out of their homes, and to show off they say long prayers. They will be judged most harshly." Jesus sat across from the collection box for the temple treasury and observed how the crowd gave their money. Many rich people were throwing in lots of money. One poor widow came forward and put in two small copper coins worth a penny. Jesus called his disciples to him and said, "I assure you that this poor widow has put in more than everyone who's been putting money in the treasury. All of them are giving out of their spare change. But she from her hopeless poverty has given everything she had, even what she needed to live on."

—Mark 12:38–44

In first-century Judaism, scribes were devout, pious persons who devoted themselves to worship and to studying Torah. Because they were professional interpreters of Scripture, their advice was sought by anyone aspiring to be part of God's realm.

Yet Jesus is as critical of the scribes as they are of him. Specifically, he accuses them of cheating "widows out of their homes" (presumably to fill the temple coffers). One day they "will be judged most harshly" (v. 40).

Widows occupy a special place in God's concern for justice, making it all the more sad that the scribes, the interpreters of religious law, are defrauding those whom the religious law charges them to protect.

Jesus notes the rich placing their big gifts in the temple treasury, but he gives special notice to the poor widow who drops in two coins, all that she has. In noticing the widow, Jesus is once again focusing on "the least of these." And as he frequently does, Jesus turns the tables, seeing those who appear to be great as small and exalting those who are unimportant in the eyes of the world.

But more is going on in this episode than Jesus commending an older woman for exemplary stewardship. Jesus charges that the temple in Jerusalem is corrupt. In Mark 13:1–2, Jesus's disciples admire the temple, but Jesus says that the temple will be torn down, stone cast from stone. The disciples look at the religious establishment and see beauty to be admired; Jesus sees corruption and disobedience of God's will.

Jesus sees with sadness the woman's gift together with the hypocrisy and corruption of the scribes.[1] He laments that the religious leaders will squander the poor woman's gift, even though she is giving them all that she has. Through her self-sacrificial gift, the old woman is unknowingly propping up a corrupt government-religious apparatus. But Jesus sees and Jesus knows: the widow is a lover of God who is being victimized by those who are charged by God to be her protectors.

Though this older woman is not prominent in the eyes of the world, Jesus sees her, in all her innocence and goodness. And though corrupt religious leaders prey on the goodwill of people, especially poor (older) people, God sees and knows and is working to end this corruption.

Maybe Mark tells this story as encouragement not to give up. Even though the elderly poor may be vulnerable to corrupt political, economic, and religious systems, God sees and is moving on their behalf.

In this passage, there is a word of comfort for the vulnerable, including the aged, who put their trust and their treasure in religious institutions and those who lead them. There is also a warning for the powerful, who busily administer systems that dominate the poor and the vulnerable, particularly if the systems are God's. God takes sides. Corrupt, insensitive religious leaders, beware.

The church must engage the rising storm of aging, not only because it is a demographic, social crisis but also because we are mandated by Jesus Christ to align ourselves with the disempowered against the powerful, particularly in the church.

It is my passionate conviction that Christian congregations are the ideal location for equipping disciples for their vocations and for helping people negotiate life's transitions, especially the stage of life called aging. I therefore agree with Rowan Greer that "the best care we can give the aged is, when possible, to use their gifts and to love them for what they can give. This means trying to avoid segregating the aged or at least seeking to mitigate the isolation as much as we can. We can strive to enable the aged to keep on serving, to be needed."[2] No better place for this to happen than in your church and mine.

Christian Community

Numerous studies show that older adults who are involved and embedded in vibrant social networks tend to have better physical and mental health than individuals who do not enjoy such close ties.[3] A congregation—those assembled by Jesus Christ to be his physical, bodily, communal presence in the world—is a natural place for significant human social interaction. Neal Krause, who cites many studies on the good effects of church involvement, defines church-based social support as "the emotional, tangible, and spiritual assistance that is exchanged among people who worship in the same congregation."[4] In a culture plagued by detachment, loneliness, and separation, the church's practices of community have become a great gift we have to offer the world.

The church should do all it can to help older people socialize, even when they have mobility challenges. In communities where there is a lack of public transportation, a church van ride service can be a godsend. Technology, such as the internet, provides a potential means of social connection for seniors and enables homebound people to be connected to the church. It is now possible for every congregation to have contact with homebound members and for seniors to keep up with the life of the congregation through social media.

Congregational culture must move from seeing the aging as those who lack—no job, declining health, slackening intellectual interest—to those who have attained a special status in the Body of Christ, those who have acquired (according to Jimmy Carter) a set of virtues and who have the gifts of longevity, life, and time for service to others.[5] People over sixty-five spend more time volunteering than any other age group, and over 45 percent of all older volunteers help others through religious organizations.[6]

While extolling the joys of life in community, we ought to acknowledge that negative interactions and unpleasant social encounters can erode the physical and mental health of older people.[7] Krause characterizes deleterious exchanges in the church as "disagreements, criticism, rejection, and invasion of privacy" and "excessive helping as well as ineffective helping."[8] When one has spent years supporting a congregation, watching it slowly decline or be torn apart by controversy is no fun. My own denomination is closing hundreds of churches every year. When a church closes, usually the only members left to be displaced and to grieve the death of a congregation are the elderly.

If older people are very loyal to their congregation, negative interactions with people in the congregation can be quite painful. Having lost some of the social connections that brought joy in earlier days, they find negative interactions, division, bickering, and squabbling within the church to be particularly difficult.[9]

Intergenerational Interaction

One of the gifts of many churches is intergenerational interaction. We have become an age-segregated society in which the aging members have no vital role to play (unlike an agricultural society where there is still much for elders to contribute, such as child rearing). Close to 7 percent of the American elderly live in either residential facilities or senior living communities.[10] These communities provide advantages for older people, like an increased sense of security, neighbors, friends, social interaction, recreation, proximity to care-givers, and freedom from being an undue burden on loved ones. Yet age-segregated communities also have disadvantages, including a lack of diversity of interaction, high cost, and the illusion that one is really living independently.

A serious drawback of these communities is that death is ever present. One reason Christian funerals ought to be held in a church is that mortuaries and funeral homes, or chapels in nursing homes, have only one association: death. When a Service of Death and Resurrection occurs in a church, it takes place amid a host of intergenerational memories from the entire life cycle: baptism, marriage, Sunday worship.

The church is in the meaning-making, meaning-receiving business. A primary instrument of meaning-making is the church's worship. Every Service of Christian Marriage is not just about a bride and a groom. The service is preparation for marriage and supports those already married. In similar ways, the Service of Death and Resurrection is not just for the immediately grieving family. It is also education and preparation for grief and dying for all those present. For the elderly who are in the immediate crisis of aging, as well as for the young who are preparing to age, the intergenerational nature of the church is a great gift.

In Jesus Christ, the Fourth Commandment to honor our elders is not abrogated, but it is reformed through a creative restructuring of the family. Through the baptismal reformation of the family and the formation of a new and distinctive people called the church, the command to honor our elders is expanded, and we are given responsibility for people beyond the bounds of our own generation.

The best way to form intergenerational bonds in the church is by working together across generations in ministry and letting the bonds arise out of our shared work in Christ.

In a study of twenty black congregations in Philadelphia, John Morrison found that these congregations refused to organize themselves by rigid age designation and separation. Members of the church had difficulty telling whether a member was under or over sixty-five. Young people were given the opportunity at an early age to participate in key governing groups. Functional rather than chronological criteria were used to define membership in various cohorts, and there was much age diversity within the majority of the church's gatherings. Morrison believes that "development of specific senior citizens groups within churches may not be wise. In fact, a number of pastors [whom he studied] felt that age designations or age segregated programs were inherently problematic and should be avoided."[11]

At the conclusion of a congregational study on forgiveness in Jesus's name, I noted how our study had been enriched by having three or four generations of Christians in the discussions. Younger members of the group tended to think of forgiveness as mostly a matter of "not being overly sensitive when somebody does something wrong to you" and of "not making too big a deal out of it." The middle-aged members of the group questioned the practicality and workability of an ethic of forgiveness. "Is Jesus serious?" one asked. The older members of the group agreed to the great difficulty of forgiveness but also told some moving stories about why forgiveness is essential in order to live life without great sadness.

"When I get to be your age," said a younger participant, "I hope I'll be half as honest as you are about how hard it is to follow Jesus."

"I'm sure you will," said the older person. "God has done so many good things in your life already."

A prophetic witness of the church in our day is to push back against our society's tendency to age-segregate and to show how Jesus Christ gives his followers the ability to appreciate one another, to give and to receive differing gifts from one another, and to take responsibility for one another across generations.

Erik Erikson said that successful aging calls for the cultivation of "generativity," the ability to stay reasonably productive and connected to others who are busy engaging with the challenges of life.[12] George Vaillant says that a key factor in the well-being of those over sixty-five is frequent contact with younger generations. It is particularly life-giving for the elderly to be invested in the lives of younger people outside their biological families, supporting and admiring their work, which will outlive them.[13]

Senior Appreciation Sunday is usually a testimony to a congregation's marginalization of the elderly. If aging is a lifelong task for everyone in the church and if all our days, particularly our last, are occasions for witness and ministry, then treating aging as a particularly tragic time of life or a moral achievement worthy of unusual honor can be counterproductive to fostering a Christian sense of aging. The church owes its aging more than honor; what the elderly most need from the church is continued deployment in mission.

The prophet Micah, condemning Israel's corruption, saw tensions between parents and children as a symbol of Israel's apostasy: "For the son treats the father with contempt, / the daughter rises up against her mother" (7:6 NRSV). Malachi, on the other hand, looked forward to a time when God's faithful people would be united across the generations:

> Look, I am sending Elijah the prophet to you,
>   before the great and terrifying day of the LORD arrives.
> Turn the hearts of the parents to the children
>   and the hearts of the children to their parents. (4:5–6)

Churches need to provide multiple opportunities for interaction between older members and youth. The young must come to terms with the elderly among them and be honest about the ways they may fear being around aging bodies. People skip funerals, warehouse the elderly, and avoid visiting nursing homes in the unacknowledged hope that by evading the aging, they won't have to face the truth that they too are moving inexorably toward their end. "You shall be as I," warns a New England tombstone, reason enough for the young to be wary of the old. As Augustine said, *timor mortis* (fear of death) is the driving force behind much of humanity's best and worst.[14]

In a culture in which there is widespread age segregation and growing friction between Boomers and Gen Xs, Millennials, and iGens, an intergenerational church is a gift to both young and old. A chief role of a pastor is to be a community person whose task is to constantly look for opportunities for unifying practices. Effective pastors encourage the cohesion of the community and work for the inclusion of all. Here are some ways a church can encourage intergenerational interaction.

- Many aging adults must eat alone; mealtimes are often the loneliest times of their day. Church members can regularly eat together with age groups mixed.

- Baptism and confirmation offer important opportunities for intergenerational relationships. Mentor-based confirmation programs are a grand opportunity to pair an older, more experienced Christian with a novice Christian.[15]
- When someone moves into a nursing facility or into a room at a retirement center, representatives from the congregation can visit and offer a blessing.
- When a pastor or lay caregiver visits the elderly in a nursing facility, they can bring young people along.

Many older adults spend a great deal of their time alone, more so than at any other time in their lives. Self-concern, a challenge at any time of life, can be magnified. Bernice Neugarten sums up her research on personality change in older adults: "Although there are important differences between men and women as they age, in both sexes, older individuals seemed to move toward more eccentric, self-preoccupied positions."[16] Some among the elderly feel that if they do not care about themselves, no one will. Depression, anxiety, and difficulty with problem solving can arise out of older adults' excessive self-absorption. Intergenerational connections can help older adults move beyond unwarranted self-concern.

The Christian faith helps to shift the focus away from self. The best ministries of the church draw people out of themselves in engagement in mission, thereby giving people the means to be concerned about someone other than themselves.

Mary Pipher warns that at whatever age we find ourselves, we all have a stake in helping the elderly: "Soon our country will be avalanched by old people, and those people will be us. In a few decades, our solutions to the dilemmas of caring for our elders will be applied to our own lives. The kindness, the indifference, the ignorance, and the wisdom will be passed on. The more we love and respect our elders, the more we teach our children to love and respect us. The more we think through problems today, the more organizational and cultural structures will be in place to handle our generation's needs."[17]

In giving, we receive. By modeling healthy intergenerational interaction—teaching the young how to respect and cherish the old and teaching the old how to support, teach, and encourage the young—the church embodies its Golden Rule and shows the world that Christ is capable of creating a truly beloved community.

The Gifts of God for the People of God

Among the potential gifts of life within a Christian congregation are these:

- The church helps us think about matters that, for all sorts of reasons, are difficult to think about in this culture.
- The church provides a lifetime of preparation for death.
- The church is a primary location where we deal with losses and seek healing for the pain of loss.
- The rituals of the church provide for the public processing of our fears and our sorrows, setting our anxieties in the context of the full sweep of the Christian faith.
- The church calls certain people elders, potentially making the church a place where there is contact with and formation by the wisdom of the ages as young and old minister to one another.
- In the church's rituals and liturgy we actively practice and encourage remembrance and lovingly guard and reiterate tradition as we corporately submit to judgment by and the witness of the saints.
- The church is where we tell stories, giving and receiving testimony from the living and the dead about the way to a life worth living.
- The church is a location for engagement in confession, forgiveness, and reconciliation.
- The church is a place of thoughtful, imaginative reflection on our lives and our future.
- The church is where ordinary people receive their vocations, where we accept our assignments in the mission of Jesus Christ, and where we are commissioned to participate in his moves in the world that he is saving.
- The church can be a place where we bring some of our self-deluding, self-absorbed nostalgia under control. We can rise

above sappy, sentimental fictions of the human condition and learn to tell the truth about ourselves and the world.

- The church is where we find grace and Sabbath rest and are lifted above our desires to produce, to control, to consume, and to be independent.

- The church is where we are given the grace and the time to look back and sense Providence at work and where we take time to attend to one another, including the elderly.

- The church is where, in a world of lies, we learn to tell and to hear the truth and to be reconciled to God, to ourselves, and to one another.

- In the church we help others name and claim their God-given gifts as the old encourage the young to discover and affirm their vocations.

What the Church Needs to Do for the Aging

"Our congregation is located in a huge retirement area," a young woman said. "We've never been members of such an active church. We've got dozens of ministries—food distribution, medical transportation, emergency assistance, tutoring of kids, study groups around the clock, six services of worship every week. I can't believe our good fortune at having such a great place to be the church. The need is so obvious, the gifts so evident, and the opportunities for mission so boundless because we have so many retired folks with the time and the talents to lead us!"

Only the church would look on the storm of aging, the exponential increase in the number of elderly, as a grand opportunity to be the church. Christians are called not just to be forgiven and saved but also to be in mission. Here are some ways the church can be in mission to the aging.

Support Caregivers

Millions of Americans are engaged in caregiving. Many of these caregivers report that caregiving is the major source of stress in their lives. In fact, the challenges of caregiving have been called "the twenty-first century's greatest test of character."[18] Families may want to help elderly family members negotiate the challenges, but aging can be hard on everybody. One family out of four is caring for an older relative. For the first time in history, many middle-aged people will have more parents alive than they have children.[19] Our freedom to move to other parts of the country for jobs or lifestyle means that we are geographically dispersed. "Every weekend I spend more time getting to my parents to check on them than I spend time with them," a woman in my congregation lamented.

The average age for caregivers is forty-nine.[20] Many in the "sandwich generation"—those caught between caring for aging parents on one end of the life spectrum and raising children on the other—find large portions of their lives consumed by caring for vulnerable parents who once were their stalwart protectors. Caregivers feel guilty for taking time away from their children to care for an aged parent. Should the resources that the caregiver has saved for future retirement be depleted by paying for the care of an aged parent?

The stress associated with caregiving often comes not simply from the demanding tasks of care but also from the lack of value and reward our culture places on caregiving. The incentive to get out of bed, to start moving, to make a list, and to feel a sense of responsibility can be rewarding for those who find meaning in their caregiving roles. Sometimes the challenge is to find a way to make involuntary caregiving become, to some degree, voluntary—to discover joy in service to another in need.

Few of us can choose the older adults for whom we provide care; nor can we choose who will be our caregivers, which serves as a reminder that our lives are not constituted by our choices but by God's grace. Therefore, a theological task for many of us is to see the aging for whom we care as gifts and to see those who care for us in our need as God's gifts to us.[21]

Whereas most congregations attempt to be in contact with their elderly members, few churches have active programs of support for those who give care to the elderly. Every church ought to know who is functioning as a caregiver. Then to support them, church members can honor the caregivers' around-the-clock care by offering a few hours of respite. Members of the church can also provide assistance such as shopping, cooking, cleaning, and banking, along with social activities such as visiting, listening, and sharing feelings.

A couple years ago, when I was teaching in Australia, the country was rocked by the news that an elderly woman with Alzheimer's had starved to death after her caregiver husband had suffered a stroke and died. They had been dead for days when they were found, sitting together at their breakfast table. He was her sole caregiver and even though the couple was affluent and neighbors had offered to help, he had refused because he felt that his wife's care was his sole responsibility as a loving husband.

Caregivers may be reluctant to ask for help and neighbors may be reluctant to insist on giving help, but things ought to be different in the Body of Christ.

Provide Retirement Planning

By the late twentieth century, the average number of years of retirement prior to death had increased from three to fifteen.[22] Many of us will spend more time in retirement than any previous generation.[23] Retirement, whether voluntary or involuntary, can be a useful shock that jolts us into the realization that we are indeed aging. In retirement, we are given the gifts of being able to grow, to embrace new possibilities, to find jobs that better fit our gifts and life experiences—in short, to make the transition from (as one rabbi put it) "age-ing to sage-ing."[24]

Unfortunately, planning for retirement has been monopolized by financial advisors. What if, once a year, the church sponsored a celebration/retreat for those who had reached sixty-five? Pastors could also help people devise a theological plan for retirement that answers questions like, "How will I spend my time with God?" and "What new spiritual disciplines will I assume?"

I say again: one can retire from a job but not from Christian discipleship. Those who reach sixty-five should receive pastoral guidance about their vocation in retirement. Wasting the precious time we have been given by being preoccupied with ourselves cannot be an option for those who aspire to age like Christians. "I no longer have a job, so I can no longer be the person I was; who is God calling me to be now?" is an appropriate question for those moving into retirement.

Discuss Legacy

A moral test of a life well lived and a dying well done is how we make out our will. To whom will we give the material things we've accumulated? George Vaillant says that whereas the task of young adults is to create biological heirs, the task of old age is to create social heirs.[25] Because we have here no "permanent city" (Heb. 13:14), it is fair to ask, "What will we leave behind?" Communally, socially, doxologically, what will be our bequest? Every church stewardship program should have a component that encourages legacy planning, giving that keeps on giving after we're gone. If we have loved a congregation in life, we can ensure that its ministry remains vibrant by our gifts to it in our deaths.

As Christians, we are under obligation to be good stewards of our material goods. "We give Thee but Thine own, whate'er the gift may be. All that we have is Thine alone, a trust, O Lord, from Thee," my childhood church taught us to sing as we brought the offering plates forward on Sunday. Each Sunday's offering is a dress rehearsal for our final offering, handing over to God everything we once thought was ours. If only King Lear could have seen that his power and possessions were not his to dole out in order to sustain his privilege but rather God's gifts entrusted to him for a season and then returned to the giver.

A historian of my church explained our decline: "In its first hundred years, the Methodist Church built institutions to help other people's children. In their second century, Methodists mainly supported institutions to benefit their own families." Most of us in the top decile of economically privileged Americans will leave little behind to anyone other than our children. What we've accumulated could do much good for a wider set of heirs.

John Wesley said famously, "Gain all you can, save all you can, give all you can," with Wesley's emphasis decidedly on "give all you can."[26] Wesley received much money from his publications but made certain that he died poor and directed that only paupers be allowed to carry his coffin to his grave. Thus he taught his heirs a valuable lesson in legacy.

Plato advises that the most enduring legacy is another person similar to ourselves.[27] As Christians, may we aspire to leave a public witness of our gratitude for the life we were given, the part we played in God's work, our courage in the face of death, and our steadfast hope in the triumph of Jesus Christ.

Eugene Bianchi says that the best legacy we can leave our children "is a personally lived lesson about facing old age and death with courage and grace."[28]

Promote Vocation

We Christians are those who do not have to fabricate their identities by ourselves. We are Christians because we have been summoned, commissioned, enlisted, called by God to join in God's work in the world.

There are interesting parallels between late adulthood and adolescence. The identity question—"Who am I?"—that occupied much of anguished adolescence can also be asked with intensity and poignancy in the later adult years. The question can be particularly painful for older adults who have already achieved certain things and lived enough of life for personality to be well developed if not downright ossified. The person who had a ready answer to "Who am I?" now must answer, "I know who I have been, but who am I now?"

The vocational assertion "It is God who hath made us and not we ourselves" (Ps. 100:3 KJV) sounds odd, schooled as we are in the contemporary American fiction that our lives are our possessions to use as we choose. Yet as Christians, we assert that we are derivative, contingent, created by a God who breathes life into mud (Gen. 2:7) and loans breath only for as long as God wills.

At any time in life, but especially in one's last decade, the typical American question "What should *I* do with *my* life?" is the wrong question. Modernity compels us to write the story that defines who we are, to choose from a variety of possible plots to make a meaningful existence. Christians believe the proper question is not "What do *I* want to do?" but rather "How is God calling me to service?"

Theologian Karl Barth characterized vocation as a "place" where we are met by God's summons. "In any moment we meet the call of God anew, and, hence, in every moment it is as it were, 'just setting out.'"[29] Vocation's power, said Hermann Hesse, is when "the soul is awakened . . . so that instead of dreams and presentiments from within a summons comes from without" and "presents itself and makes its claim."[30] To be a Christian is to be called from without, to be externally authorized, given a role to play in God's salvation of the world. That we are not self-made implies that we are God's property to be called into service as God pleases.

In the New Testament, "calling" or "vocation" refers to discipleship rather than to employment. We can be called to eternal life (1 Tim. 6:12), into fellowship with Christ (1 Cor. 1:9), out of darkness into light (1 Pet. 2:9), and into right relationship with God (Rom. 8:30), but not to a career. Paul was a tentmaker (Acts 18:3), but nowhere is Paul "called" to be a tentmaker. Tentmaking put bread on the table, justification enough for Paul to give it his best. For those who have overly invested themselves in careers or even in parenting a family, the last years of life present an opportunity to recover the joy of more fully giving themselves to discipleship.

Vocation is what God wants from us, whereby our lives are transformed into a consequence of God's redemption of the world. Jesus Christ chooses not to work alone. In vocation, God attaches us to projects and purposes greater than ourselves. Look no further than Jesus's disciples—remarkably mediocre, untalented, lackluster yokels—to see that innate talent or inner yearning has less to do with vocation than God's desire to redeem lives by assigning us something to do for God. As Jesus succinctly says, in a verse that must be rediscovered at every stage in life, "Ye have not chosen me, but I have chosen you, and ordained you, that ye should go and bring forth fruit" (John 15:16 KJV).[31]

While there are good reasons for older people to retire from their careers or the labors of parenting, there's no theological justification for them to think that their responsibilities to Jesus are fulfilled so that now they can focus only on themselves.

As we have noted, aging is often accompanied by much loss. Sometimes God calls us from our losses and helps us regather our sense of purpose in order to move into a new future with reformed identity and purpose. Grieving our losses can be a call for prayer and reflection to make sense of our situation and undertake the tough vocational work of reconstructing our identity, role, and relationships.

"My children are pressuring me to move. They're concerned that with my bad hearing, it's dangerous for me to live alone," the retired English professor shouted at me across her living room during a pastoral visit.

By the end of the afternoon, I sat in another living room with a father and his teenaged son in crisis. The single parent had a demanding job. When he came home at the end of the day, his son's blaring rock music was more than he could take. They argued about everything and were miserable.

"I wish I could move out of this house!" the son wailed.

"You and me both," sneered the beleaguered father.

Under the influence of the Holy Spirit I said, "Wait. I may have the answer to your problems."

After a bit of negotiating, the next day the teenager moved in with the elderly retired professor. "Your music won't bother me," chuckled the woman. "I'll turn off my hearing aid and you rock away! Now that you are living with me, I can stay in my home."

The three of them—father, son, and older friend—sat together in church on Sunday. These kinds of intergenerational relationships embody God's vision for healthy relationships in church.

We must honestly confront the clash between the American Zeitgeist and the Christian story about aging, nourishing the notion that at any stage in our lives we are still called to discipleship and community. Continuing discipleship usually requires transformation and change in order for us to be faithful. God has created us as people who have a need to serve, a compulsion to give. As Christians, we are commissioned to be Christ's representatives in the world. For the church to be complicit in taking away people's responsibility is sad.

Coach Mike Krzyzewski—a faithful Catholic—spoke at the Duke University retirees' luncheon. He said, "As I look around this room, I see people who were masters in physics, housekeeping, neonatal care, plumbing, roofing. Such wisdom is gathered here. What valuable experience!"

Coach K paused for a moment, leaned into the microphone, and said,

> Now you owe us! I've got a friend who coaches a team where only two out of his fifteen players know their fathers. Look, people, the American family is in a mess. We need you. It's not good enough for you to sit back and say, "I raised my kids. I'm not looking after someone else's." Your wisdom and experience are valuable community resources!
>
> Now, I've got notepads and pencils at every table. Write down what you are going to do to make Durham a better place, something you are good at that the world needs. Those of you who are already working to give back to the community, you write down what you are doing. We are going to sit quietly for a moment while you write this down. Then we'll collect them. Now!

For me, it was a grand moment of Christian vocation.

A woman in my church who suffered a terribly debilitating nerve disease asked me, "I wonder what God has in mind for me now?"

"Er, what do you mean?" I asked her awkwardly.

"I don't get out anymore," she said, "but, preacher, I'm perfectly capable of using a telephone." Each morning I would give her a list of people to call—visitors from the previous Sunday, people in the hospital, students away at college, committee members who needed to be reminded of meetings. I ordained her the Minister of Telephoning.

Mary despised being relegated to a nursing home when she broke her hip and was forced into a wheelchair for the rest of her days. She had been a high-powered business executive in her previous life.

She told me, "So I said to myself, 'You've spent your whole life rushing about, never time to sit and talk and listen to anybody. Now's your chance.'"

She asked the nurses to give her a list of folks who were lonely and who had few visitors. Each day Mary "goes to the office" by wheeling herself up and down the halls, knocking on doors, and asking people if they would like a visit. Now's her chance.

Martin Luther's conviction that every station in life can be a calling from God should be applied not to our careers but to the stage of life in which we are living. One could make a case that the Christian calling to stewardship, hospitality, compassion, advocacy, and social justice can be exercised better during the last years of life than in prior stages. How wonderful to be able to say with satisfaction, after having exchanged a job for a vocation, "This is who I am. For this, I was made."[32]

When I led a delegation from our church to participate in the Moral Monday demonstration at the state capitol, I was a bit disappointed that the only people I could assemble were retired. Then I thought, who is better able to see the ravages of bad government or who is freer to risk arrest at a demonstration protesting a miserly state budget than retired school teachers and public servants?

Though we don't know many details about that place where God bids us in our ending, in our dying we can be hopeful that the God who constantly, resourcefully called us in life will continue to call us in our deaths. As we prepare for death, we have a last opportunity to ask, "What is God doing with me now?"

John Wesley, founder of the Methodist movement, bragged, "Our people know how to die!"[33] Dying well means witnessing to God's grace right to the end and gratefully remembering the manner and the good of one's life and for the church to remember us in the same way.

Grow in Grace

In my own Wesleyan tradition, we stress the power of God's grace working in us, at every time of life, to make us better than we could be without God. Grace is the power of God that enables us to have a more faithful life than we would have had if our lives had been left up to us. The great Wesleyan theological achievement was linking justification to sanctification, salvation by grace to growth in grace, promising not only rebirth but also continuing reconstruction. A living God keeps remaking us even when we think we are done. No one ages out of the adventure of Holy Spirit–induced growth in grace.

Rembrandt painted a picture of his elderly mother. The old woman is not sitting quietly, gazing out the window as the world passes by. She is intently studying a large open Bible.[34] In most congregations of my acquaintance, older adults are the majority of those in study groups. Their participation is not due simply to their having more time on their hands. Aging provokes an intellectual crisis that calls for reframing, rethinking, and reconsidering the concepts and the principles that guided us during earlier years of our lives. The church can be a great location for thoughtful, intellectual exploration. Older adults need to be students not only because of the intellectual requirements for successful aging but also because we want to "grow in every way into Christ" (Eph. 4:15).

Mainline Protestant church decline is due in part to a corporate failure of intellectual nerve, amnesia regarding the core affirmations of the faith, and distraction that allows the nonessentials to crowd out the essentials. Christians need to read, think, and study their way out of this malaise.

At a church I recently visited, a woman (about my age) invited me to attend her Sunday school class.

"We are studying Mark 1:1 today," she said.

"Just the first chapter of Mark's Gospel?" I asked.

"The first verse of the first chapter," she responded. "At last we have the time to go deeper, verse by verse."

Offer Learning Opportunities

Churches ought to offer a class titled "Thinking like Christians about Aging." Class content could be derived from the chapters in this book. Here is a suggested learning plan using each of the book's chapters and specifying some possible learning outcomes.

1. Aging with Scripture

    Participants will know the way that Scripture is honest about both the challenges of aging and the gift of a long life. They will note the roles that the aged sometimes play in Scripture.

2. The Storm of Aging

    Participants will be able to cite two or three reasons aging presents great challenges for living in the last years of life. They will have greater appreciation for the increasing challenge that longevity presents for our society.

3. Retiring with God

    Participants will better appreciate the blessings of retirement and cite three or four trials of retirement after a career.

They will come to view retirement as a test of character and an opportunity to see their lives as God's continuing creations.

4. Successful Aging

Participants will be able to define unrealistic fantasies of aging and to list three or four proven biological, social, and theological contributors toward successful aging.

5. With God in the Last Quarter of Life

Participants will be able to cite two or three core Christian affirmations and practices that enable them to think more truthfully and fruitfully about aging in specifically Christian ways.

6. Growing Old in Church

Participants will gain new appreciation for the ways in which their congregation can be a valuable resource and support for persons preparing for and living through aging as well as how their congregation can prepare younger members for aging.

7. Ending in God

Participants will have renewed confidence that God goes with them as they live through the last days of their lives. They will be encouraged to see the Christian affirmations about death and life after life as key theological support for facing the end with hope.

What the Aging Need to Do for the Church

"Much will be demanded from everyone who has been given much, and from the one who has been entrusted with much, even more will be asked" (Luke 12:48). We are created to be givers. Those who are given the gift of advanced years are called primarily to see themselves not as passive patients but as agents, not as receivers but as givers, not as burdensome but as responsible.

A congregation ought to frame its work as a ministry *of* older adults rather than a ministry *to* older adults. Some aging adults (not all, but perhaps more than we admit) have the gifts of time, financial resources, patience, wisdom, experience, and skills that are badly needed among many in the congregation and in the congregation's neighborhood.

"I look on myself as the senior networker," said the woman who was her congregation's coordinator of senior ministry.

"What's a 'senior networker'?" I asked.

"Well, I begin with the slogan that older adults are not primarily to be served but to serve. We have more important things to do than a fall trip to the mountains to see the leaves change. I tell them, 'If you want trips with old people, see a travel agent. The church is entrusted with a more pressing mission.'

"So I network, trying to help all the older adults discover and affirm their God-given missions."

"Such as?" I persisted.

"Such as putting a young man who has been out of work for a year with two of my older men who were business guys in their former lives. I told them they have to see this thing through until Thomas lands a job. I have a woman who was a master tailor teaching three of our younger women how to sew. I even have three older adults—all recovering alcoholics—on call as the pastor needs them to care for alcoholics in the congregation."

She is my model for older adult ministry.

In the New Testament, widows are given the task of prayer. A 1999 study revealed that of the 98 percent of older adults who pray, most pray for the well-being of others, especially family members. Of these, 95 percent believe their prayers are answered.[35] The church is a community of prayer, work that nearly all of the aging can do well.

I know a church that has been in the urban church slide for decades. Today that church is beginning a near-miraculous turnaround. The pastor gives all the credit for the congregation's revitalization to a group of older women, the Wednesday Morning Prayer Circle. They had risked praying, "Lord, what can we do to give our church a future?"

The Lord directed them to start a free child care ministry at the church on Friday nights. They put a big sign in the church's yard: "Free, Expert Child Care, Fridays 5–11 p.m." The children get a meal prepared by the women, games, bedtime stories, and movies, and the parents get a free night out as well as a welcoming encounter with the church.

"Those Friday evenings have been used by God to transform our church," said the young pastor.

When the Alabama legislature passed the meanest anti-immigration law in the country, one of the churches that urged me to sue the legislature in the name of Christ (we won our suit, by the way) was a church in a central Alabama town. A group of older members in the church ran a program for latchkey kids who could go to the church in the afternoons and do homework and have fun until their parents got off work. Most of the students spoke Spanish. The program was run by a retired high school Spanish teacher who, though she was not a church member, was recruited by her friends in the church to oversee the program.

The law made the program illegal; it was unlawful to "harbor" or "transport" undocumented people. I'm proud to say that, even in Jeff Sessions's state, these courageous women said, "We aren't stopping this ministry for anybody. What are they going to do? Jail a bunch of eighty-year-olds?"

Here are some other ways aging adults can help the church.

Witness

While it's true that aging can be a time of worry, regret, and loneliness, our last decades can also be, by the grace of God, a time for heightened Christian witness. All Christians are called to testify to who God is and to what God is up to in the world, and to encourage others to hitch on to that work. Yet those who are "old and gray" can have a particular witness:

> They will bear fruit even when old and gray;
>   they will remain lush and fresh in order to proclaim:
>   "The LORD is righteous.
>   He's my rock.
>   There's nothing unrighteous in him." (Ps. 92:14–15)

Older members can "remain lush and fresh." Why? "In order to proclaim." God gives some a blessed, fruitful old age, not simply for personal satisfaction and contentment but for witness.

I still remember being challenged in one of my first congregations by the witness of an older man who never missed a Sunday. Each week he hobbled in on crutches and took his place toward the front of the church. I once asked him, "Tom, do you have much trouble with pain?"

"Son, I haven't been without pain for the last thirty years after my accident. It takes me at least an hour of prayer and dogged determination just to get out of bed each morning."

Until that moment, I had never heard Tom speak of his pain.

Self-restraint is a virtue when talking about our problems. Effective Christian witness requires skill to know when to speak and when to withhold our speech. When we obsess over our aches and pains, our limited horizon is exposed, showing that our main concern is ourselves. We seniors, like Tom, must be stewards of our pain and misfortune and must show how, even in our pain, God can still be praised.

"I woke up this morning feeling unwell," I told Tom one Sunday, "head hurting, not wanting to get dressed and come to church. Then I remembered you would be sitting in the first pew to the right. Here I am!"

I overheard an older woman saying to another, "My deafness has gotten so bad that I can't make out a word of the sermon."

"If you can't hear, then why do you come?" asked the other person.

"I come to be an example to the rest of you," she said with a giggle. "At least my deafness is physiological. How about you? Ever had trouble listening to the preacher's sermons?"

When one of our older church members was diagnosed with lung cancer, a younger member attempted to console her by asking, "You've lived such a good life. Are you angry with God for this bad luck?"

"Angry with God?" the older woman snapped back. "I'm the one who smoked a pack a day for forty years. I hope God isn't too angry with me!"

Oh, the blessed witness of the elders who "remain lush and fresh in order to proclaim."

The biblical stories of Jacob and Esau at the approach of Isaac's death (Gen. 27) and of Joseph and his brothers at the time of Jacob's death (Gen. 49) show that sometimes at the end family fault lines are rent when suppressed tension built up over years is made undeniable and visible. Some older adults can witness that it is possible, even at the end of life, to engage in the tough work of reconciliation and forgiveness. There is often a great deal of regret and loss among the elderly, but there is also time for fixing broken relationships and setting things right before the end.

A fair question is "What is the work you need to do before you die?"

When I have been asked if people should plan their funerals, I have sometimes said, "Sure. Plan your funeral. But more important is doing any unfinished business with others so you can have a peaceful passing." Much grief is due to regret over fences not mended and relationships left broken.

It's possible to do work in our later years that we neglected when we were young. It is never too late to say to another, "Can you forgive me?" "I forgive you," "Thank you for what you gave me," "I love you," or "Goodbye." Closure heals relationships, provides opportunities to be obedient to Christ, and enables us to experience the reconciling Holy Spirit in our lives.

Sometimes finishing the work of our lives is difficult because well-meaning palliative caregivers have medicated us into a stupor. It's important for us to say, even in our pain, to those who would offer us mind-numbing drugs, "I want some of my pain assuaged, but I also need to be as conscious and alert as possible to accomplish the work that I need to do before I go."

Elderly people can also be witnesses by reminding us that aging and death are not the worst things that can happen to us. Worse is to die without having lived. Jesus speaks (especially in the Gospel of John) of the walking dead who have yet to live. In the face of death, Christians assert that while death is the final enemy, it is not our most daunting test; life with God is the challenge.

"Let us describe that task of the old, . . . as a task of *witness*," says Oliver O'Donovan. "The old have neither to conform to the young nor to resent them by standing at a distance, but to be themselves *before the eyes of* the young, to live and to die as they have lived hitherto, to make available to the young the experiences they have lived through authentically, standing where they have always stood on important matters, cheerfully adapting themselves, as best they can, in unimportant ones. That is what the young need of them."[36] Let our prayer be that of the psalmist:

So, even in my old age with gray hair,
don't abandon me, God!
Not until I tell generations about your mighty arm,
 tell all who are yet to come about your strength,
 and about your ultimate righteousness, God,
because you've done awesome things! (Ps. 71:18–19)

May God give each of us time enough to tell generations about God's mighty arm.

Step Aside

Earlier we discussed the witness of old Elizabeth and Zechariah and Simeon and Anna. Note that they began the story of Jesus with their prophetic vision of God's future. Then what did these elders do? They moved out of the way and are never heard from again. Let us elders take these exiting matriarchs and patriarchs as exemplars.

At a clergy conference, Lauren Winner, associate professor at Duke Divinity School, and I were asked by an older clergyperson, "Why doesn't the church do a better job of retaining and utilizing our older clergy to serve some of our smaller parishes?"

As an older clergyperson, my heart resonated with this priest's plea. But I remember Lauren responding with, "I'm sorry. I know so many young Episcopal clergy who have finished seminary and have been waiting for years to be sent to a parish. I really hope that some of you clergy who have enjoyed years of fruitful ministry will now consider stepping aside."

The young have the responsibility to enter life and take hold of the world, faithfully fulfilling God's commission. The old have the obligation to be supportive of those who now bear the major burdens of leading the church. We should wish them well . . . and then step aside.

We can witness to what we have found to be true. We can sympathize with them as they take up the burdens we once bore, offering suggestions and encouragement when asked. But we must remember that they don't live in the same world in which we lived. Though they work at many of the tasks we tackled, they must work differently. They must dismantle some of the things we so lovingly constructed.

Through them, God may solve problems we attempted but failed to solve. They are not merely continuing the work we began. The world changes. Christians, young and old, all serve a living God with whom we have more future than past, a God who refuses to stay stuck in the status quo or hemmed in by what was done before. That is why some of the most important service the old can render the young is to step back, bless them, and say, "It's yours now."

The young have their hands full. A chief vocation of the aging is to stand beside the young, to offer them encouragement and consolation as they take up their duties in life's first half. Because sometimes the years bring wisdom, perspective, a sense of proportion, and reliable knowledge, the old feel more self-assurance than the young and therefore can stand beside them during their times of uncertainty.

I know a church that was having a rough time financially. At an anxious meeting of the board, one of the older members gave a brief history of the congregation, highlighting five financial crises (worse than the present) over the congregation's past fifty years. After hearing the history, the pastor said, "Thanks for reminding us of our past. Folks, we're encountering nothing today that God hasn't brought us through before!"

Frustrated by our lack of control of our lives, we older folks must not attempt to control the young or vainly try to live vicariously through them by dominating their lives. We must step aside, trusting that God will lead a new generation in the church.

Grandparent as a Vocation

Of those sixty-five and older, 80 percent have grandchildren. One-third of these older Christians say that grandparenting is the most satisfying aspect of their lives.[37] And yet grandparenting has its challenges. Successful grandparenting typically depends on parents who value having grandparents in their children's lives. In my last church, the major task being faced by many older members was caring for grandchildren who, for various reasons, had been handed off to the grandparents to raise.

Grandparents can provide a constant, reliable safety net for grandchildren, giving them much-needed emotional support in their negotiations and tensions with their parents, teachers, and peers. Grandparents also give children a sense of security and stability when dealing with divorce, parental substance abuse, or parental illness or death.

Grandparents are quite naturally called to be storytellers. As teachers and mentors, grandparents are a link with a family's past, giving children a wider picture of the world and its meaning, and a richer array of life options, than may be available through parents. Deuteronomy praises the truths that grandparents can teach their progeny:

> Remember the days long past;
>   consider the years long gone.
> Ask your father, he will tell you about it;
>   ask your elders, they will give you the details. (32:7)

In the early days of my ministry a young woman tearfully told of her discovery of her husband's infidelity that occurred at a business convention. "I'm leaving him, of course, even though he says he's sorry and will never do it again. I can't trust him. First I'm going to tell my sainted grandmother. This will just break her heart." Two days later the she was back in my office. She surprised me when she told me, "Well, I've decided to try to forgive Jim and see if we can pick up and move on from here."

"What led you to change your mind?" I asked. And she told me this story:

> I told my grandmother, "I've got something to tell you that will be a shock. Jim has committed adultery." Grandmother said, "Not a shock to me. Many men go crazy at Jim's age. Is he repentant? Has this happened before?"
>
> "Grandmother!" I said. "I never would have thought that you would justify infidelity."
>
> "Didn't say I justified it," she said. "Just said that if Jim's repentant, if you think you can find a way to forgive him, then maybe you should. Men can be much better husbands after this sort of thing."
>
> I told her that I was surprised she would even suggest that I take Jim back. That's when she said, "I took your grandfather back twice after he had played the fool. Sometimes marriages are better after this sort of thing. Ours sure was."
>
> "*Grandfather!*"

Some of the wisdom that grandparents have to teach is unpleasant for the young to hear. There are times when the elderly, without even trying, pronounce prophetic judgment on the superficial values of our society, its infatuation with youth, its denial of death, its ethos of self-help, its idolization of stuff, its elevation of individualism, and its myths of self-sufficiency. Elders have a nasty habit of putting uncomfortable questions to the young: What's the point of your life? Will accumulation of all this stuff really lead to happiness? Amid the ravages of time and mortality, what are you giving your life to that will last?

Above all, grandparents have a responsibility, by virtue of their baptism, to pass on their Christian faith to their grandchildren. If it is true that many elders have a heightened spiritual sense in their later years and that many middle-aged persons are so consumed with careers and other life projects that they withdraw from religious activity, then it is especially important for the elderly to instruct their grandchildren in the faith. As a college chaplain, I noted that the majority of college students who identified themselves as Christians testified that those most responsible for bringing them into the faith were their grandparents.

Sinners as we are, even a great good like grandparenting can be perverted if it stands between us and God or distracts us from the rest of our Christian vocation. Some of the elderly are living diminished lives because they feel no concern for anyone but their grandchildren. To the dear person who brags, "I would do anything for my grandchildren," the church must say, "That's not good enough."

The rite of baptism is upfront in proclaiming that progeny is not limited to biological heirs. In most services of baptism, members of the congregation present candidates, and the entire congregation pledges to take responsibility for the newly baptized in this strange, countercultural family called church. Grandparenting can be a vocation that goes beyond biology.

I once served a congregation in which the majority of members were over sixty-five. We set out to attract younger adults who were moving into our changing neighborhood.

"Do you miss your grandparents?" I would ask as I visited the young adults in the apartment building near the church. "We've got grandparents to spare."

Our church was pleasantly surprised that a number of young adults gravitated toward our congregation, saying, in effect, "Growing up is too tough without some help from those with gray hair." We began asking young adult visitors to Sunday dinner. Those meals proved to be one of the most important doorways into our church and a major means of evangelism.

In that same congregation, I asked the evangelism committee, "Who are the people in this town who need us?" One of our older members answered, "Young couples with babies." She explained, "Young couples are having babies, and they know so little about babies. They also don't have grandparents nearby, so there's nobody to adore the babies."

After much discussion, we selected a couple in their seventies to be our baby visitors, and they called on every baby who was born in a mile radius of our church. When a baby was brought home, within a week or two, this couple would show up on the doorstep, saying, "We understand that your lives have been turned upside down by God's gift." Then after admiring the newborn, they would say, "Our church makes young children a priority. Here's a Bible storybook. It's never too soon to read Bible stories to your baby. Here's a brochure about what our church is doing. We want you to know that our church is here to help you be the parents this adorable child deserves."

The baby visitors were our most successful evangelistic program. At least twenty young couples joined our church as fruit of this ministry. Half of the couples were unmarried. A fourth of the babies were being raised by single parents. That program reminded us and our neighborhood that Christian baptism is a sign of our responsibility for one another, the first step into the church's countercultural family.

In a church in North Carolina, the pastor invited those who were to be baptized to come to the front of the sanctuary. A mother and two little girls came forward. "This is Alicia and her daughters, Juanita and Loris," said the pastor. "We met them through our migrant hospitality ministry." As the mother gave her testimony, the pastor translated into English: "When we came to America, we realized that people didn't want us here. We heard what the president said on TV. But the Methodists welcomed us. Back home, we had never heard of

Methodists. John and Mary got me a great job in town. Elizabeth even helped me get a car to go to work. Alice's grandchildren got the kids settled in their new school. We couldn't have made it without you."

The pastor said, "I'd like to ask everyone who brought this dear family to us to come down and join us at the baptistery." Eighteen people—all of them older adults—surrounded the family. Grandparenting had become a vocation.

Elder-Friendly Churches

Here are some appropriate questions (gleaned from James Houston and Michael Parker) that churches should ask themselves:

- What are the demographics of our congregation?
- What specific programs are offered for seniors?
- Have we partnered with other community agencies for senior care?
- Do we have a system for supporting senior caregivers?
- Are we using technology to keep in close contact with our seniors?
- Is our church truly accessible for those with mobility issues?
- Do we have multiple ways of encouraging intergenerational interaction?
- Do we have nutrition programs for seniors?
- Do we have a sound system for the hearing impaired?[38]

What if your church had a trained and vetted ombudsman for the aging? People who are moving through the health care system need advocates, interpreters, those who can support them in an often impersonal system.[39] A well-informed congregational advocate for the elderly who is knowledgeable about care options and who has established relationships with care facilities, including hospice, in the community can reassure older persons and support their caregivers.

A study in the 1980s showed that 39 percent of Americans with serious problems are apt to seek help from a member of the clergy;

clergy are the major mental health counselors.[40] Older women are more likely than either older men or younger people to turn to clergy for help with personal problems.[41] It therefore behooves every pastor to be knowledgeable about the predictable crises of the aging. Even more important than knowing when and how to help is realizing when and how to refer people to other professional caregivers such as counselors, psychologists, psychiatrists, physicians, and social workers.[42]

Because older adults often feel vulnerable and fearful, and therefore concerned about their safety, the security of church spaces is an important concern. We expect churches to be safe sanctuaries for our children; how about for the elderly? The AARP website has practical ideas for improving the safety of older adults (www.aarp.org).

Many older adults suffer from dementia. To make the church more elder-friendly, churches should seek education on how to work with people with dementia. Fortunately, the National Institute on Aging has a helpful website with concise information about Alzheimer's disease and how to make a church friendly and safe for those with dementia diagnoses (www.nia.nih.gov).

Many congregations lack a compelling sense of mission. The presence of elderly members or the elderly in the community near the church offers a great opportunity for congregational revitalization and engagement in mission. Here are some other ways to make a church elder-friendly.

- Designate a trained coordinator of older adult ministry to organize and deploy people of all ages in ministry to and with older adults.
- Recognize and affirm caregivers for the elderly in a congregational worship service.
- Start a caregiver support group. Keep an active list of caregivers and offer them periodic relief from their work as well as resources and ideas to help them with the burdens of care they have assumed.
- Conduct a survey of those in the congregation and the neighborhood who may benefit from Meals on Wheels and other support from the congregation.

- Have regular luncheons for older adults and their caregivers.
- Offer transportation for older adults for every church function, and establish a vetted team of informed volunteers who are available to provide transportation, oversight, help with medical visits, and friendly conversation to the elderly.
- Offer help; don't wait for elders to ask.

Worship and the Elderly

Much of the church's worship, like the second half of life, is a time for reflection and assessment. That is one reason the elderly have a high level of church attendance. Many older adults enjoy the opportunities that worship affords for fellowship and for contemplation and review. So many of Jesus's parables are stories of judgment when the master asks simply, "What have you done with what you have been given?" (see Matt. 25:14–30). Aging can be a time of reflection and solitude, a time of looking back on one's life and taking stock, which is not always a wholly pleasant undertaking. And yet, with the perspective of time, some of the things that caused anguish in an earlier stage of life can be seen as relatively unimportant. Some of the good fortune that was hardly noticed is now assessed to have greater significance.

Guilt for things done and left undone can plague older adults. Some look on the behavior of adult children and second-guess their parenting. Others regret the accumulated mistakes they have made.

Regular use of prayers of corporate confession and assurances of pardon and forgiveness is a sign to the elderly that the church is there to relieve one encumbrance of old age: burdensome regret.

Christian worship not only expresses our deepest beliefs and most ardent aspirations. As we are busy praising God, we are also being formed and reformed by God in our worship. Some of our perfectly normal, natural reactions can be disciplined in worship by the formative power of the Holy Spirit and the Word of God. Even though we tend to be self-centered, it is possible to be changed, to some degree, by allowing the Holy Spirit to work in our lives and by submitting ourselves to Scripture.

"You can't teach an old dog new tricks," libel often applied to older people, is challenged by the Christian faith and its views of conversion and sanctification. God's transformative work in us does not end at sixty-five. Nor does aging mean that we are unable to learn new patterns and assume new habits. One of those habits may be the habit of altruism. It is possible for a person who has been greedy and self-centered to see, in later years, the true worth of things and become more giving. The person who has felt financially insecure and therefore has been relentlessly acquisitive may come to realize that now they have fewer pressing commitments and are free to be more generous, to invest in causes that benefit others, to increase their range of commitments, to rise above fixation with personal needs, and to feel the pain of others as vividly as their own.

In sermons, preachers should take care not to use words that demean or stereotype the aging. Much of Protestant worship is dominated by words, so those who are incapable of using words well are at a disadvantage in worship. It is not surprising then that the Eucharist—full of actions too deep for words—is important in nursing homes or that patients who are verbally dysfunctional suddenly join in when "Amazing Grace" is sung or Psalm 23 is recited. They are drawing deep from the well within, showing habits of faith that were accrued over a lifetime.

Music takes us deeper than the verbal, drawing us out of our loneliness as we join with others in singing the same words and notes. A service in which all the music is exclusively of one generation to the neglect of others falls short of the wonderfully intergenerational quality of Christian worship at its best.

"Do you love and miss your grandparents?" I used to ask students at Duke University Chapel. "Well, here at the chapel we'll introduce you to your great-great-grandparents! This morning we will enjoy one of Isaac Watts's greatest hits and submit ourselves to the wisdom of dead people who can deepen your prayer life."

When a church I once served installed a drop-down screen in the sanctuary for the display of the words to our songs and other acts of worship, I expected pushback from some of our older members.

"For the first time in a long time I can actually see the words to the hymns!" a vision-impaired octogenarian said as she gave encouragement to the church's reach toward a new generation.

SEVEN

Ending in God

Before we end, let's talk about the end, eschatology, last things, our future with God. We use "the end" in at least two ways. *End* means "final"—the last chapter of the story, when the game is over, the last breath, *finis*. *End* can also mean *telos*, "purpose"—the result of our work, the meaning of the story, the goal of our efforts, the point of it all, our ultimate destination. The Westminster Confession asks new Christians, "What is the chief end of humanity?" What's our purpose, the meaning of our lives? The Christian is taught to answer, "To glorify God and to enjoy God forever." We are here on this earth for no better reason than the glorification and enjoyment of God, in all life's ups and downs, so that one day, by God's grace, we may enjoy God forever.

Our Last, Best Hope

We older adults have an advantage over younger cohorts when it comes to pondering matters of the end. Death denial is widespread; our rituals for dying are in disarray. The traditional Christian Service of Death and Resurrection is replaced with a bouncy, upbeat Celebration of Life where we are urged to laugh about the foibles of the deceased, an exercise that all too easily degenerates into corporate make-believe that death has not really occurred.

Youth infatuation and cosmetic surgical intervention to cover the physical effects of aging indicate that we find it difficult to think about aging's most daunting task—dying. We ask, "How can creatures so wonderful as we be finite?" Eat this food, follow these principles, live by this regimen twice daily, take this pill, work out, endow an institution—live forever. Even with our culture's pervasive denial, those of us past sixty-five have fewer means of evading the reality toward which we are moving. We know in our more truthful moments that over even well-lived lives, the most faithful friendships, our greatest artistic and cultural achievements, the most abstemious of diets, and the institutions that we've built and supported hovers a solemn warning: *this too shall pass.*

The satanic promise to Adam and Eve in the garden ("You will be like God" [Gen. 3:5]) is the lie of immortality. I'm sorry, but there is no path to godlike immortality. Only God is eternal. Surely, this is a truth that's more comprehensible to the old, whose myriad of little losses culminate in the big loss: *thanatos.*

Too bleak? To Christians are given the resources to be honest about mortality. As Paul says, "We always carry Jesus' death around in our bodies so that Jesus' life can also be seen in our bodies" (2 Cor. 4:10). Our lives are not our own. We live each day not for ourselves, and we die on our last day not unto ourselves. Christians are able to be so brutally honest about death, utterly realistic about the lethal human situation, because we are so optimistic about the power of God in Christ. We have confidence in the promise of God's steadfast love, which overcomes death and the forces of evil. God is life and light, and in the resurrection of crucified Jesus Christ, our final foe is defeated: *Thanatos* vanquished by *Christos.*

The Christian faith has its origins in a cemetery and the jolt of God's surprise move—the resurrection of the body of crucified Jesus. The church originates in the shock of Jesus Christ returning to the same disciples who deserted him and fled into the darkness. They left Jesus's body at what they thought was the end; he bodily returned to them that they might begin again and become his body in motion, his church. It's not over with us and God until God says it's over. If we are to have life beyond the limits of this passing, earthly life, our hope is that the God who raised Jesus will bring us along with him into eternity. Our hope is that Jesus Christ not only is raised to everlasting life but also, in an amazing act of love, reaches out to us in our mortality and takes us along for the ride. Jesus Christ refused to be raised alone. As John Calvin put it, "Christ rose that he might have us as companions in the life to come."[1]

Eternal life means being welcomed by God into God's existence, being subsumed into God's story, taking our place in God's reign, and being adopted into the communion of saints. This enlistment into God's story begins whenever we join in God's work in the world. Our days with God in this life are a foretaste of our end.

Revelation comes at the end of the Bible and the beginning of the church. The Revelation to John seems to be a vision of a person whose world was coming apart, whose horizon was ending. And yet as so often happens with human history in the hands of redemptive God, the pain of the present moment is radically transformed by God's intervention. The Lamb—slaughtered, crucified, and bloody—reigns at the center of heaven, ruling from the throne.

> Then I saw a new heaven and a new earth, for the former heaven and the former earth had passed away, and the sea was no more. I saw the holy city, New Jerusalem, coming down out of heaven from God, made ready as a bride beautifully dressed for her husband. I heard a loud voice from the throne say, "Look! God's dwelling is here with humankind. He will dwell with them, and they will be his peoples. God himself will be with them as their God. He will wipe away every tear from their eyes. Death will be no more. There will be no mourning, crying, or pain anymore, for the former things have passed away." Then the one seated on the throne said, "Look! I'm making all things new." (Rev. 21:1–5)

In the Revelation, John gives us a poetic, visionary celebration that makes a strong theological claim: God has triumphed. At last God has what God wants when "every knee should bend . . . and every tongue should confess that Jesus Christ is Lord" (Phil. 2:10–11 NRSV). The One whom the world pushed out of the world on a cross has risen and returned in order to transform the world. The creation that God began in Genesis is brought to its fulfillment. The glorification and enjoyment of God, for which we were created, glimpsed only momentarily here, will there be our full-time job. We will forever whoop it up in the choir with no more pressing business than praise (Rev. 19).

In my pastoral experience, people don't think much about the end or eternal life or heaven until they must. Perhaps this is as it should be. Jesus urged us not to overly concern ourselves with tomorrow but rather to focus on the blessings and the work that God gives us today (Matt. 6:25–34). People in power, people who are in good health, those who are young and have an expansive future ahead of them need not think much about finitude or spend much time pondering what's next. However, for people over sixty-five, thinking about our end is not an optional activity. Our bodies, the deaths of our friends and family, and the sense that the world we inhabited is slipping away speak to us of our finale.

Earlier we discussed the vocation of older adults to witness and to give testimony. Matters of the end, mortality, and the hope of eternal life may be the distinctive content of elders' unique witness. We older adults can be salt and light in a death-denying culture as we testify that life after life is not simply a future expectation; it can be a present reality.

Eschatological hope for God's great victory at the end empowers us now. This life is preparation and training for whatever life is to come, though the resurrection of the body and eternal life are gifts of God. All along life's way we can experience the redemptive, resurrecting work of the One who raised crucified Jesus from the dead. There is no situation at any time in our lives so bleak and tragic as to be immune from God's saving work, no tragedy so frightful that it is beyond the reach of a redemptive God. Though full emancipation takes place only after we have departed this life, this life, here and now, can be transformed by knowing our end in God.

I asked the director of an inner-city ministry that cares for the bodily and the spiritual needs of deeply impoverished older adults how she has kept going against all odds, performing this demanding work for decades. She replied, "I try to take the long view. We're in a battle here, but I know who will finally win the war. God isn't forever mocked. I'm giving my people a foretaste of what God has in store for them. That keeps me going."

As Jesus said, "I came so that they could have life" (John 10:10). Because we anticipate that time, that place when "the kingdom of the world has become the kingdom of our Lord and his Christ, and he will rule forever and always" (Rev. 11:15), we don't lose hope. Affirmation of God's ultimate triumph is among the most politically charged and economically relevant of Christian doctrines, especially for those over sixty-five. People who are dealing with unfinished business, unrealized expectations, and worry over the current state of affairs need to hear the evangelical word that the last chapter will be written by the God who raised crucified Jesus from the dead.

Jesus defeated death, triumphed, and, in an amazing act of grace, takes us along through this veil of tears all the way to whatever realm God has in store for us in eternity. Our belief is not based on some naive fantasy about the future but on the solid evidence of God's love that we've experienced here. Because God in Christ has gone to such extraordinary lengths to get to us in this life, we cannot believe that God will fail to reach out to us in death.

> I believe that the present suffering is nothing compared to the coming glory that is going to be revealed to us. The whole creation waits breathless with anticipation for the revelation of God's sons and daughters. Creation was subjected to frustration, not by its own choice—it was the choice of the one who subjected it—but in the hope that the creation itself will be set free from slavery to decay and brought into the glorious freedom of God's children. We know that the whole creation is groaning together and suffering labor pains up until now. And it's not only the creation. We ourselves who have the Spirit as the first crop of the harvest also groan inside as we wait to be adopted and for our bodies to be set free. We were saved in hope. If we see what we hope for, that isn't hope. Who hopes for what they already see? But if we hope for what we don't see, we wait for it with patience. (Rom. 8:18–25)

When it comes to our ultimate destiny, our fates are in the hands of a merciful God who is God of the just and the unjust, who makes his sun to shine on the undeserving heads of both the righteous and the unrighteous (Matt. 5:45), whose Son came to save sinners, only sinners. In death, we are forced to fall back on the everlasting arms, compelled to admit just how little we are able to control our lives. If the elderly are closer to their end, if their daily lives give them a foretaste of their contingency and mortality, then it can truly be said of them that they are turning and becoming as little children, not too far from the kingdom (18:3).

Revelation says that in paradise, when the kingdom of heaven comes on the earth in its fullness, there will be no church (21:22). Why? Presumably, we won't need the church to train us to be at peace with God and our neighbors. We won't have to content ourselves with glimpses of eternity in Sunday worship. We will have arrived. The people of God will shine like the sun. We will see God, not as through a mirror dimly but face-to-face (1 Cor. 13:12). The veil of mortality will be lifted, and our always aging, wasting bodies will be made whole. That stunning, glorious light who is God Almighty and the Lamb will effusively shine on us (Rev. 21:22). We will then see God fully and see ourselves as we have been created from the beginning to be. We will be home.

Until then, we who are aging (that's all of us) can see our lives with God in this present moment, in whatever circumstance we find ourselves, as preparation to be with God forever.

The Christian Funeral

Recently, I attended the funeral of a longtime friend. He was active in his church and was a vibrant, though not unquestioning, believer. The preacher at his funeral seemed unaware—or unconcerned—about my deceased friend's relationship with Christ or his commitment to God's work. She went on at length about my friend's personal charm and his cooking ability.

"And best of all, he was a grandfather who truly loved his grandchildren." Wow, what a remarkable achievement. Take that all you unaffectionate grandfathers!

It was an unfortunate funeral sermon, not only because it was poorly delivered and badly constructed but also because it lacked theological interest or substance. Furthermore, all my friend's virtues and vices are quite beside the point at the end. The sermon implied that our hope in life, in death, in any life beyond death is in our charm, good cooking, and affectionate grandparenting. Jesus Christ failed to win even a cameo role in the sermon, and everybody left the service with the impression that the Christian faith has nothing to say at the time of death than what the world already knows.

We must recover the funeral as a multigenerational, church-wide event, not as a private service for the family. Everyone who attends a funeral either is in the acute crisis of grief or is preparing for grief, so a funeral is for the whole church, an opportunity for the church to say to itself and the world what it believes about God. A funeral is a service of corporate Christian worship, a time for education and testimony, and also a prophetic witness to a world that denies death or settles for sentimental bromides and superficial banalities.

In funerals, we give back to God one whom God gave to us. Funerals are a time of memory and gratitude for a life, but our most grateful remembering should not be about the alleged achievements of the deceased. Funerals should stress the ways that we are cherished and owned by God. "If we live, we live for the Lord, and if we die, we die for the Lord. Therefore, whether we live or die, we belong to God" (Rom. 14:8). In life, in death, and in life beyond death, we are claimed, named, cherished, and commissioned by God.

Carole Bailey Stoneking says that what we most need in assessing successful aging is not "optimism, but hope."[2] Our hope is not found in what we can remember and recall about the deceased but rather in God's remembering of us all. Throughout the Scriptures, God is said to remember individuals and Israel (Gen. 9:16; 19:29; Lev. 26:42–43; Ps. 105:42). To say that God remembers is to praise God's fidelity. Humanity forgets; God remembers. Whether in life or in death, we are not forgotten.

Thomas Long and Thomas Lynch, our best contemporary interpreters of Christian funerals, say that the purpose of funeral rites is "to get the dead where they need to be and the living where they need to be."[3] The body is lovingly carried to its final resting place, and the mourners return to life without the bodily presence of the deceased. The funeral is an affirmation not only that in grief we need others to help us deal with our grieving but also that the person who died was a member of the Body of Christ, a social being who had a claim on us and on whom we were dependent. By God's grace alone, the funeral is not only a service of death but also a service of resurrection, an affirmation that whether we live or die, we are God's.

"Remember your creator in the days of your youth," counsels Ecclesiastes 12:1 (NRSV). It's also important to remember God in your last days when so much is forgotten. Let us remember God in our last quarter of life as we ponder the theological significance of our aging, because there is no one to lift the heaviest burdens of aging but God. As I admitted at the beginning of this book, when all is said and done (sooner rather than later for this septuagenarian), there is no cure for the ills of mortality and finitude but God. In our ending, as in our beginning, may we live in such a way that in our coming and going, in our living and dying, we are able to join the church in proclaiming, "Thanks be to God!"

Notes

Introduction

1. Will Willimon, *Accidental Preacher: A Memoir* (Grand Rapids: Eerdmans, 2019), 201–2.

2. T. S. Eliot, *Love Song of J. Alfred Prufrock*, in *The Complete Poems and Plays: 1909–1950* (New York: Harcourt, Brace, 1952), 7.

3. Dylan Thomas, "Do Not Go Gentle into That Good Night," Poets.org, February 1, 2015, https://www.poets.org/poetsorg/poem/do-not-go-gentle-good-night.

4. Marc Freedman, "The Boomers, Good Work, and the Next Stage of Life," in *MetLife Foundation/Civic Ventures New Face of Work Survey* (San Francisco: Civic Ventures, 2005), 4, http://www.encore.org/files/new_face_of_work[1].pdf.

5. Cited in Lloyd R. Bailey, *Biblical Perspectives on Death* (Philadelphia: Fortress, 1979), ix. See also Augustine, "Sermon 51," in *St. Augustine: Essential Sermons*, trans. Edmund Hill, ed. Boniface Ramsey (Hyde Park, NY: New City Press, 2007), 63–75.

6. David S. Potter, *The Roman Empire at Bay: AD 180–395* (New York: Routledge, 2004), 18.

7. Data from the US Bureau of the Census 1984 as interpreted in Sheldon S. Tobin, James W. Ellor, and Susan M. Anderson-Ray, *Enabling the Elderly: Religious Institutions within the Community Service System* (Albany: State University of New York Press, 1986), 5–6.

Chapter 1: Aging with Scripture

1. Robert Browning, "Rabbi Ben Ezra," Poetry Foundation, https://www.poetryfoundation.org/poems/43775/rabbi-ben-ezra.

2. Billy Graham, *Nearing Home: Life, Faith, and Finishing Well* (Nashville: Nelson, 2011).

3. Graham, *Nearing Home*, 8.

4. Richard B. Hays and Judith C. Hays, "The Christian Practice of Growing Old: The Witness of Scripture," in *Growing Old in Christ*, ed. Stanley Hauerwas, Carole

Bailey Stoneking, Keith G. Meador, and David Cloutier (Grand Rapids: Eerdmans, 2003), 11.

5. Hays and Hays, "Christian Practice of Growing Old," 11.

6. Martha C. Nussbaum and Saul Levmore, *Aging Thoughtfully: Conversations about Retirement, Romance, Wrinkles, and Regret* (New York: Oxford University Press, 2017), 10.

7. Mike Featherstone and Mike Hepworth, "Images of Ageing in Social Gerontology," in *The Cambridge Handbook of Age and Ageing* (Cambridge: Cambridge University Press, 2005), http://www.credoreference.com/entry/cupage/images_of_ageing_in_social_gerontology.

8. John Calvin, *Institutes of the Christian Religion*, ed. John T. McNeill, trans. Ford Lewis Battles, LCC (Philadelphia: Westminster, 1960), book 1, chap. 6, §1.

Chapter 2: The Storm of Aging

1. William Shakespeare, *As You Like It*, act 2, scene 7, lines 140–65.

2. David Wright, "Lines on Retirement after Reading Lear," in *In a Fine Frenzy: Poets Respond to Shakespeare*, ed. David Starkey and Paul Willis (Des Moines: University of Iowa Press, 2005), 211.

3. William Shakespeare, *King Lear*, act 1, scene 1, line 90.

4. Shakespeare, *King Lear*, act 1, scene 1, line 40.

5. Shakespeare, *King Lear*, act 1, scene 1, line 297.

6. Shakespeare, *King Lear*, act 4, scene 7, lines 58–59.

7. Shakespeare, *King Lear*, act 1, scene 1, lines 313–16, 317–18.

8. Shakespeare, *King Lear*, act 3, scene 3, line 22.

9. Shakespeare, *King Lear*, act 5, scene 3, lines 394–95.

10. Martha C. Nussbaum and Saul Levmore, *Aging Thoughtfully: Conversations about Retirement, Romance, Wrinkles, and Regret* (New York: Oxford University Press, 2017), 17.

11. Nussbaum and Levmore, *Aging Thoughtfully*, 11.

12. Shakespeare, *King Lear*, act 1, scene 4, line 158.

13. "A person's characteristics tend to become more accentuated as his life goes on." Paul Tournier, *Learn to Grow Old*, trans. Edwin Hudson (Louisville: Westminster John Knox, 1991), 118.

14. Stanley M. Hauerwas, *A Community of Character: Toward a Constructive Christian Social Ethic* (Notre Dame: Notre Dame University Press, 1981).

Chapter 3: Retiring with God

1. Richard Rohr, *Falling Upward: A Spirituality for the Two Halves of Life* (San Francisco: Jossey-Bass, 2011), xii.

2. Rohr, *Falling Upward*, 26.

3. Rohr, *Falling Upward*, xiii–xiv.

4. Rohr, *Falling Upward*, 45.

5. Rohr, *Falling Upward*, 48.

6. Oliver O'Donovan, "The Practice of Being Old," in *Church, Society, and the Christian Common Good: Essays in Conversation with Philip Turner*, ed. Ephraim Radnor (Eugene, OR: Cascade, 2017), 208.

7. Rohr, *Falling Upward*, 138. Using James Fowler and Richard Rohr (rather uncritically), Terry Nyhuis urges congregations to move from being closed, limited, and divisive "First Half Churches" to being more open, accepting, and embracing "Second Half Churches." Terry L. Nyhuis, "Aging Baby Boomers, Churches, and the Second Half of Life (Challenges for Boomers and Their Churches)" (DMin diss., George Fox University, Newberg, Oregon, 2016), 65–77, 81–87, http://digitalcommons.georgefox.edu/dmin/136.

8. "Suicide," National Institute of Mental Health, last updated April 2019, https://www.nimh.nih.gov/health/statistics/suicide.shtml.

9. PK, "Average Retirement Age in the United States," *DQYDJ* (blog), September 27, 2019, https://dqydj.com/average-retirement-age-in-the-united-states.

10. PK, "Average Retirement Age."

11. James Hollis, *Finding Meaning in the Second Half of Life: How to Finally, Really Grow Up* (New York: Gotham Books, 2005), 260.

12. Hollis, *Finding Meaning*, 14–15.

13. Hollis, *Finding Meaning*, 149–50.

14. "Wealth Inequality in the United States," Inequality.org, Institute for Policy Studies, https://inequality.org/facts/wealth-inequality.

15. Social Security Administration Fact Sheet, https://www.ssa.gov/news/press/factsheets/basicfact-alt.pdf.

16. Martha C. Nussbaum and Saul Levmore, *Aging Thoughtfully: Conversations about Retirement, Romance, Wrinkles, and Regret* (New York: Oxford University Press, 2017), 182–83.

17. Nussbaum and Levmore, *Aging Thoughtfully*, 182–83.

18. "Topic No. 751 Social Security and Medicare Withholding Rates," IRS.gov, last updated August 23, 2019, https://www.irs.gov/taxtopics/tc751#targetText=Social%20Security%20and%20Medicare%20Withholding,employee%2C%20or%202.9%25%20total.

19. Robert S. Pfeiffer, "Entitlement Spending," February 17, 2019, federalsafetynet.com/entitlement-spending.html.

20. Kenneth Calhoun, "Nightblooming," *Paris Review* 189 (Summer 2009), https://www.theparisreview.org/fiction/5930/nightblooming-kenneth-calhoun.

21. Barbara Boxer, "A Segment of Former U.S. Senator Barbara Boxer's Retirement Speech," *LA Times*, February 3, 2017, video, https://www.latimes.com/politics/92496452-132.html.

22. See my proposed "Liturgy for Retirement" in John H. Westerhoff III and William H. Willimon, eds., *Liturgy and Learning through the Life Cycle*, rev. ed. (Akron, OH: OSL, 1994), chap. 12, pp. 149–52.

23. Preached in Duke University Chapel, July 13, 1997.

24. Shakespeare, *Macbeth*, act 5, scene 5, lines 30–31.

25. Reynolds Price, *A Whole New Life: An Illness and a Healing* (New York: Atheneum, 1994).

26. Price, *Whole New Life*, 183.

27. Price, *Whole New Life*, 183.

28. Erdman Palmore, *The Honorable Elders: A Cross-Cultural Analysis of Aging in Japan* (Durham, NC: Duke University Press, 1975).

29. Thomas Naylor and William H. Willimon, *The Search for Meaning* (Nashville: Abingdon, 1994).

Chapter 4: Successful Aging

1. James O'Neill, *The Third Pill*, BBC, August 31, 2018, https://www.bbc.co.uk /programmes/b0bgmxh3.

2. Christiane Northrup, "Goddesses Never Age: Your Best Years Are Ahead," Christiane Northrup, MD, October 6, 2016, https://www.drnorthrup.com/goddesses -never-age-best-years-ahead/.

3. Cicero, "Cato Maior de Senectute," 35–36, quoted in Martha C. Nussbaum and Saul Levmore, *Aging Thoughtfully: Conversations about Retirement, Romance, Wrinkles, and Regret* (New York: Oxford University Press, 2017), 77.

4. James Woodward, *Valuing Age: Pastoral Ministry with Older People* (London: SPCK, 2008), 137–38.

5. J. W. Rowe and R. L. Kahn, *Successful Aging* (New York: Pantheon Books, 1998), 122–24.

6. Rowe and Kahn, *Successful Aging*, 144.

7. James M. Houston and Michael Parker, *A Vision for the Aging Church: Renewing Ministry for and by Seniors* (Downers Grove, IL: IVP Academic, 2011), 143–44.

8. Carole Bailey Stoneking, "Modernity: The Social Construction of Aging," in *Growing Old in Christ*, ed. Stanley Hauerwas, Carole Bailey Stoneking, Keith G. Meador, and David Cloutier (Grand Rapids: Eerdmans, 2003), 63–89.

9. Arthur Frank, *The Wounded Storyteller: Body, Illness, and Ethics* (Chicago: University of Chicago Press, 1995), 25.

10. A. R. Ammons, "In View of the Fact," in *Bosh and Flapdoodle* (New York: Norton, 2005), 49.

11. Donald Hall, "Affirmation," Poets.org, May 4, 2016, https://www.poets.org /poetsorg/poem/affirmation.

12. Carl G. Jung, *The Portable Jung*, ed. Joseph Campbell (New York: Penguin, 1976), 17.

13. It's interesting to see fifty-year-olds urged to do some of the adventuring that I'm advocating for sixty-five-year-olds. See Marianne Williamson, "Keep a Sense of Adventure," in *50 Things to Do When You Turn 50: 50 Experts on the Subject of Turning 50*, ed. Ronnie Sellers, 34–38 (Portland, ME: Sellers, 2005).

14. Woodward, *Valuing Age*, 12.

15. Woodward, *Valuing Age*, 53.

16. W. Daniel Hale, Richard G. Bennett, and Panagis Galiatsatos, *Building Healthy Communities through Medical-Religious Partnerships*, 3rd ed. (Baltimore: Johns Hopkins University Press, 2018), 128.

17. Woodward, *Valuing Age*, 112.

18. Woodward, *Valuing Age*, 98.

19. George E. Vaillant, *Triumphs of Experience: The Men of the Harvard Grant Study* (Cambridge: Harvard University Press, 2012), 225.

20. Vaillant, *Triumphs of Experience*, 147–48.

21. Woodward, *Valuing Age*, 205–6.

22. Roland D. Martinson interviewed fifty elders, most of whom were Christians, and assembled a revealing array of testimonies in his book *Elders Rising: The Promise and Peril of Aging* (Minneapolis: Fortress, 2018).

23. Richard Rohr, *Falling Upward: A Spirituality for the Two Halves of Life* (San Francisco: Jossey-Bass, 2011), 24.

24. Undue cheerfulness about aging pervades Richard Bimler's handbook, *Joyfully Aging: A Christian's Guide* (St. Louis: Concordia, 2012).

25. May Sarton, *As We Are Now* (New York: Norton, 1992), 1.

26. Vaillant, *Triumphs of Experience*. Vaillant assembled and summarized some of his insights derived from the Grant Study in *Aging Well: Surprising Guideposts to a Happier Life from the Landmark Harvard Study of Adult Development* (New York: Little, Brown, 2003).

27. Vaillant, *Triumphs of Experience*, 188.

28. Quoted in R. Paul Stevens, *Aging Matters: Finding Your Calling for the Rest of Your Life* (Grand Rapids: Eerdmans, 2016), 143.

29. Vaillant, *Triumphs of Experience*, 332.

30. Vaillant, *Triumphs of Experience*, 338.

31. Vaillant, *Triumphs of Experience*, 252–55.

32. Vaillant, *Triumphs of Experience*, 256–57.

33. Vaillant, *Triumphs of Experience*, 213.

34. Cf. Pope John Paul II, "Encyclical Letter *Evangelium Vitae*," March 25, 1999, para. 65, w2.vatican.va/content/john-paul-ii/en/encyclicals/documents/hf_jp-ii_enc_25031995_evangelium-vitae.html.

35. Pope John Paul II, "Encyclical Letter of His Holiness Pope to the Elderly," 1999, http://w2.vatican.va/content/john-paul-ii/en/letters/1999/documents/hf_jp-ii_let_01101999_elderly.html.

36. Thomas Moore, *Ageless Soul: The Lifelong Journey toward Meaning and Joy* (New York: St. Martin's, 2017), 3.

37. George Vaillant, *The Wisdom of the Ego* (Cambridge: Harvard University Press, 1993).

38. T. S. Eliot, "Little Gidding," in *The Complete Poems and Plays: 1909–1950* (New York: Harcourt, Brace, 1962), 142.

39. Quoted in Martinson, *Elders Rising*, 219.

40. John Stuart Mill, *Autobiography* (New York: Penguin, 1989), 115–16.

41. T. S. Eliot, "Eastcoker," in *Complete Poems and Plays*, 129.

42. William F. May, *The Patient's Ordeal* (Indianapolis: University of Indiana Press, 1991), 143.

43. Plato, *The Republic*, book 1, 329c.

44. Careen Yarnal and Xinyi Qian, "Older-Adult Playfulness: An Innovative Construct and Measurement for Healthy Aging Research," *American Journal of Play* 4, no. 1 (Summer 2011): 52–79.

45. Tom Robbins, *Still Life with Woodpecker* (New York: Bantam Books, 1980), 89.

46. Lu Yu, "Written in a Carefree Mood," trans. Burton Watson, March 2, 2009, https://poetrymala.blogspot.com/2009/03/written-in-carefree-mood.html.

47. Somerset Maugham, *The Summing Up* (New York: Doubleday & Doran, 1938), 290.

48. Mary Pipher, *Another Country: Navigating the Emotional Terrain of Our Elders* (New York: Riverhead Books, 1999), 15.

49. Malcolm Muggeridge, *The Chronicles of Wasted Time* (Vancouver: Regent College Publishing, 1999), quoted in Woodward, *Valuing Age*, 197–98.

50. William Shakespeare, *Hamlet*, act 3, scene 1, line 80.

51. On the exaggerated fears of some older adults see Will Willimon, *Fear of the Other: No Fear in Love* (Nashville: Abingdon, 2016), 21–26.

52. Willimon, *Fear of the Other*, 26.

53. Cited in Allen Lane, *Adam Smith: An Enlightened Life* (New York: Penguin, 2010), 187.

Chapter 5: With God in the Last Quarter of Life

1. Eugene C. Bianchi, *Aging as a Spiritual Journey* (Eugene, OR: Wipf & Stock, 2011), 190.

2. George E. Vaillant, *Triumphs of Experience: The Men of the Harvard Grant Study* (Cambridge: Harvard University Press, 2012), 53, 119.

3. Dan Buettner, "The Fountain of Youth," *TED Radio Hour*, May 11, 2018.

4. Vaillant, *Triumphs of Experience*, 218.

5. John Wesley, Sermon 24, "Upon Our Lord's Sermon On The Mount: Discourse Four," §I.1.

6. Simone Weil, *Waiting for God* (New York: Putnam's Sons, 1951), 31.

7. Martha C. Nussbaum and Saul Levmore, *Aging Thoughtfully: Conversations about Retirement, Romance, Wrinkles, and Regret* (New York: Oxford University Press, 2017), 17.

8. Erik H. Erikson, *Identity and the Life Cycle* (New York: Norton, 1959), 180.

9. Nussbaum and Levmore, *Aging Thoughtfully*, 25.

10. Martin Luther, *Lectures on Romans*, ed. Hilton C. Oswald, vol. 25 in *Luther's Works*, American ed. (St. Louis: Concordia, 1972), 291.

11. Christian B. Miller, *The Character Gap: How Good Are We?* (Oxford: Oxford University Press, 2017), 98.

12. Thomas Moore has a helpful discussion of anger with and among the aging in chapter 8 of Thomas Moore, *Ageless Soul: The Lifelong Journey toward Meaning and Joy* (New York: St. Martin's, 2017).

13. Dick Van Dyke, *Keep Moving: And Other Tips and Truths about Living Well Longer* (New York: Point Productions, 2015).

14. Neal M. Krause, *Aging in the Church: How Social Relationships Affect Health* (Philadelphia: Templeton Foundation Press, 2008), 145.

15. G. W. F. Hegel, *The Philosophy of Right*, trans. S. W. Dyde (Kitchener, Ontario: Batoche Books, 2001), 21.

16. "2019 Alzheimer's Disease Facts and Figures," Alzheimer's Association, https://www.alz.org/media/Documents/alzheimers-facts-and-figures-2019-r.pdf, 17.

17. James Woodward, *Valuing Age: Pastoral Ministry with Older People* (London: SPCK, 2008), 97.

18. Refrain from, "I Am Thine, O Lord," #419, *The United Methodist Hymnal* (Nashville, TN: United Methodist Publishing House, 1989).

19. Keith Meador and Shaun C. Henson, "Growing Old in a Therapeutic Culture," in *Growing Old in Christ*, ed. Stanley Hauerwas, Carole Bailey Stoneking, Keith G. Meador, and David Cloutier (Grand Rapids: Eerdmans, 2003), 90–111.

20. Mary Pipher, *Another Country: Navigating the Emotional Terrain of Our Elders* (New York: Riverhead Books, 1999), 8.

21. Woodward, *Valuing Age*, 16.

22. Richard Rohr, *Falling Upward: A Spirituality for the Two Halves of Life* (San Francisco: Jossey-Bass, 2011), 94, 110.

23. Thomas Moore has a thoughtful chapter on sexuality among the aging. See chapter 6 of Moore, *Ageless Soul*.

24. "Widowhood," Medicine Encyclopedia, 1998, https://medicine.jrank.org/pages/1840/Widowhood-demography-widowhood.html.

25. Woodward, *Valuing Age*, 121.

26. Steven Sapp, *Light on a Grey Area: American Public Policy on Aging* (Nashville: Abingdon, 1992), 49.

27. Krause, *Aging in the Church*, 207.

28. Pew Forum on Religion and Public Life, "'Nones' on the Rise: One-in-Five Adults Have No Religious Affiliation," Pew Research Center, October 9, 2012, https://www.pewforum.org/Unaffiliated/nones-on-the-rise.aspx.

29. Cited in Krause, *Aging in the Church*, 139–60.

30. Helen Rose Ebaugh, ed., *Handbook of Religion and Social Institutions* (New York: Springer, 2006), 140.

31. Vaillant, *Triumphs of Experience*, 431.

32. Vaillant, *Triumphs of Experience*, 433.

33. Vaillant, *Triumphs of Experience*, 343.

34. Vaillant, *Triumphs of Experience*, 346.

35. Harold G. Koenig and Douglas M. Lawson, *Faith in the Future: Health Care, Aging, and the Role of Religion* (Philadelphia: Templeton Foundation Press, 2004), 10.

36. Koenig and Lawson, *Faith in the Future*, 11.

37. Krause, *Aging in the Church*, 134.

38. George Barna, *The State of the Church 2002* (Ventura, CA: ISS AC AJR Resources, 2002), 79.

39. Krause, *Aging in the Church*, 16.

40. Krause, *Aging in the Church*, 153.

41. James M. Houston and Michael Parker, *A Vision for the Aging Church: Renewing Ministry for and by Seniors* (Downers Grove, IL: IVP Academic, 2011), 10. For a dramatic presentation of the horror of being both poor and old during a time of stress, see Sheri Fink, *Five Days at Memorial: Life and Death at a Storm Ravaged Hospital* (New York: Random House, 2013).

42. Vaillant, *Triumphs of Experience*, 357.

43. Preached in Duke University Chapel, December 3, 2000 (the First Sunday of Advent).

44. This sermon was dependent upon (dependency is a good thing!) a classic article by the Christian theologian Gilbert Meilaender: "I Want to Burden My Loved Ones," *First Things* (October 1991): 12–14.

45. Nussbaum and Levmore, *Aging Thoughtfully*, 120. Vaillant says that "the keys to successful aging often lie more in the realm of secular relationships" than in the religious community, though he doesn't offer any evidence for that claim. Vaillant, *Triumphs of Experience*, 278.

46. Richard B. Hays and Judith C. Hays, "The Christian Practice of Growing Old," in *Growing Old in Christ*, 15.

47. Philip Roth, quoted in David Remnick, "Philip Roth," *New Yorker*, June 4 and 11, 2018, 44.

48. Cicero, *De Senectute*, sec. 8, line 26.

49. Kafka, quoted in Remnick, "Philip Roth," 44.

50. Plato, *The Republic*, book 1, 328e.

51. Vaillant, *Triumphs of Experience*, 252.

52. Vaillant, *Triumphs of Experience*, 254.

53. Quoted in Vaillant, *Triumphs of Experience*, 249.

54. Lovett H. Weems Jr., *Church Leadership: Vision, Team, Culture, Integrity*, rev. ed. (Nashville: Abingdon, 2010), 26.

55. See the learned smackdown of the idea of progress in John Gray, *Seven Types of Atheism* (New York: Farrar, Straus & Giroux, 2018), 54–70.

56. David Matzko McCarthy, "Generational Conflict: Continuity and Change," in *Growing Old in Christ*, 226–46.

57. McCarthy, "Generational Conflict," 227.

Chapter 6: Growing Old in Church

1. André Resner Jr. says in his commentary on this passage, "I believe that Jesus's words here are to be taken as lament." André Resner Jr., *The Lectionary Commentary: Theological Exegesis for Sunday's Texts*, ed. Roger E. Van Harn (Grand Rapids: Eerdmans, 2001), 274.

2. Rowan A. Greer, "Special Gift and Special Burden: Views of Old Age in the Early Church," in *Growing Old in Christ*, ed. Stanley Hauerwas, Carole Bailey Stoneking, Keith G. Meador, and David Cloutier (Grand Rapids: Eerdmans, 2003), 37.

3. Neal M. Krause, *Aging in the Church: How Social Relationships Affect Health* (Philadelphia: Templeton Foundation Press, 2008), 148.

4. Krause, *Aging in the Church*, 146.

5. See Jimmy Carter, *The Virtues of Aging* (New York: Random House, 1998).

6. Krause, *Aging in the Church*, 147.

7. Krause, *Aging in the Church*, 152.

8. Krause, *Aging in the Church*, 156.

9. Krause, *Aging in the Church*, 172.

10. "Size and Demographics of Aging Populations," delivered at Institute of Medicine Food Forum, published in *Providing Healthy and Safe Foods as We Age: Workshop Summary* (Washington, DC: National Academies Press, 2010), https://www.ncbi.nlm.nih.gov/books/NBK51841.

11. Quoted in David Matzko McCarthy, "Generational Conflict: Continuity and Change," in *Growing Old in Christ*, 230–31.

12. Erik H. Erikson, *Identity and the Life Cycle* (New York: Norton, 1959), 211.

13. George E. Vaillant, *Triumphs of Experience: The Men of the Harvard Grant Study* (Cambridge: Harvard University Press), 135.

14. Augustine, "Sermon 161," in *St. Augustine: Essential Sermons*, trans. Edmund Hill, ed. Boniface Ramsey (Hyde Park, NY: New City Press, 2007), 221–22.

15. Will Willimon, *Making Disciples: Confirmation Through Mentoring* (Nashville: Abingdon, 2018).

16. Cited in Krause, *Aging in the Church*, 102.

17. Mary Pipher, *Another Country: Navigating the Emotional Terrain of Our Elders* (New York: Riverhead Books, 1999), 16.

18. Henri Nouwen and Walter J. Gaffney, *Aging, The Fulfillment of Life* (New York: Image Books/Doubleday, 1990), 87.

19. Pipher, *Another Country*, 15.

20. Nouwen and Gaffney, *Aging, The Fulfillment of Life*, 89.

21. The classic, Christian testimonial to the challenges of being a caregiver for someone we love who is dying is Madeleine L'Engle, *Summer of the Great Grandmother* (San Francisco: HarperOne, 1986).

22. Joan Chittister, *The Gift of Years: Growing Older Gracefully* (Katonah, NY: Bluebridge, 2008), 9.

23. A good resource for a preretirement study is R. Paul Stevens, *Aging Matters: Finding Your Calling for the Rest of Your Life* (Grand Rapids: Eerdmans, 2016).

24. Zalman Schachter-Shalomi, *From Age-ing to Sage-ing: A Profound New Vision of Growing Older* (New York: Grand Central, 1995).

25. George E. Vaillant, *Aging Well: Surprising Guideposts to a Happier Life from the Landmark Harvard Study of Adult Development* (New York: Little, Brown, 2003), 144.

26. John Wesley, "The Use of Money," quoted in *On Moral Business: Classical and Contemporary Resources for Ethics in Economic Life*, ed. Max L. Stackhouse (Grand Rapids: Eerdmans, 1995), 194–97.

27. Plato, *Symposium*, sec. 208a.

28. Eugene Bianchi, *Aging as a Spiritual Journey* (Eugene, OR: Wipf & Stock, 1987), 169.

29. Karl Barth, *Church Dogmatics*, vol. III, 4 (Edinburgh: T&T Clark, 1961), 607–8.

30. Hermann Hesse, *The Glass Bead Game*, trans. Richard Winston and Clara Winston (New York: Holt, Rinehart & Winston, 1969), 58.

31. See my more extended treatment of Christian vocation in Will Willimon, *Accidental Preacher: A Memoir* (Grand Rapids: Eerdmans, 2019), 97–116.

32. Kathleen A. Cahalan and Bonnie J. Miller-McLemore, ed., *Calling All Years Good: Christian Vocation throughout Life's Seasons* (Grand Rapids: Eerdmans, 2017), 121–22.

33. John Wesley, *Arminian Magazine* 3 (1782): 128.

34. Find this painting at https://www.theguardian.com/artanddesign/2018/jul/13/rembrandt-an-old-woman-reading.

35. Krause, *Aging in the Church*, 147.

36. Oliver O'Donovan, "The Practice of Being Old," in *Church, Society, and the Christian Common Good: Essays in Conversation with Philip Turner*, ed. Ephraim Radnor (Eugene, OR: Cascade, 2017), 214.

37. Vaillant, *Triumphs of Experience*, 60.

38. James M. Houston and Michael Parker, *A Vision for the Aging Church: Renewing Ministry for and by Seniors* (Downers Grove, IL: IVP Academic, 2011), appendix B.

39. Dr. Louise Aronson's book, *Elderhood*, begins by noting that over half of all the elderly who require hospital stays are sent there because of debilitatingly negative interactions with drugs. Her book is an impassioned plea for doctors to do a better job with the treatment of the elderly, both in prescribing medication and in directing treatment. Louise Aronson, *Elderhood: Redefining Aging, Transforming Medicine, Reimagining Life* (New York: Bloomsbury, 2019), 24, 131.

40. Krause, *Aging in the Church*, 115.

41. Krause, *Aging in the Church*, 183.

42. A congregation who wants to be active in ministering to the health needs of older adults will find informed, practical help in the standard guide to the subject,

W. Daniel Hale, Richard G. Bennett, and Panagis Galiatsatos, *Building Healthy Communities through Medical-Religious Partnerships*, 3rd ed. (Baltimore: Johns Hopkins University Press, 2018).

Chapter 7: Ending in God

1. John Calvin, *Institutes of the Christian Religion*, ed. John T. McNeill, trans. Ford Lewis Battles, LCC (Philadelphia: Westminster, 1960), book 3, chap. 25, §3.

2. Carole Bailey Stoneking, "Modernity: The Social Construction of Aging," in *Growing Old in Christ*, ed. Stanley Hauerwas, Carole Bailey Stoneking, Keith G. Meador, and David Cloutier (Grand Rapids: Eerdmans, 2003), 84.

3. Thomas G. Long and Thomas Lynch, *The Good Funeral* (Louisville: Westminster John Knox, 2013), 18.

Name Index

Scripture Index

Printed in the United States
By Bookmasters